DISCOVERING SACRED TEXTS

Series editor:
W. Owen Cole

The Christian Bible

W. Owen Cole

HEINEMANN

Heinemann Library
an imprint of Heinemann Publishers (Oxford) Ltd
Halley Court, Jordan Hill, Oxford OX2 8EJ

OXFORD LONDON EDINBURGH
MADRID ATHENS BOLOGNA PARIS
MELBOURNE SYDNEY AUCKLAND SINGAPORE
TOKYO IBADAN NAIROBI HARARE
GABORONE PORTSMOUTH (USA)

First published 1993

A catalogue record for this book is available from the British Library

ISBN 0 431 07371 6
97 96 95 94
10 9 8 7 6 5 4 3
Designed and produced by Visual Image, Street
Cover designed by Philip Parkhouse, Abingdon
Produced by Mandarin Offset
Printed and bound in China

Introduction to the series

The purpose of these books is to show what the scriptures of the six religions in the series are, to tell the story of how they grew into their present form, and to give some idea of how they are used and what they mean to believers. It is hoped that readers will be able to appreciate how important the sacred texts are to those who base their lives on them and use them to develop their faith as well as their knowledge. For this reason, members of the six major religions found in Britain today have been asked to write these books.

W. Owen Cole (Series editor)

Dedication

This book is respectfully offered to those who introduced me to the Bible; my parents and the men and women who taught me at Holme Lane Sunday School, Bradford.

Acknowledgements

During the writing of this book, many issues to which I had previously given little attention cropped up. (That is one of the enjoyably frustrating experiences of committing ideas to paper!) A number of friends helped me in my attempt to deal with them. Special thanks are due to Sue Walton and the staff of Heinemann Educational Books for transforming my manuscript into an attractive book; to the many students and children whom I have taught over the years; to Stephen Barton, Rabbi Douglas Charing, Reverend Donald Johnson, Ruth Mantin, Douglas Scrimgeour, and especially to Joy Barrow. By reading through the original manuscript she helped me to make a number of improvements and avoid a host of errors. Inevitably some faults will remain; they are mine alone. I hope that users of this book will point them out to me.

No one can succeed without the support of those who love them. Once again I thank Gwynneth, my wife, for the most valuable help of all.

The Publishers would like to thank the following for permission to reproduce photographs: Ancient Art and Architecture Collection pp.8, 19, 33, 37, 39; Andes Press Agency/Carlos Reyes p.46; Tristan Boyer p.4; British Library p.31; Carlisle Museum and Art Museum p.12; J. Allan Cash Ltd pp.6 bottom, 15, 16, 17, 22, 23, 26; Keith Ellis p.6 top; Glasgow Museums: Art Gallery and Museum, Kelvingrove p.29; Sonia Halliday Photographs pp.9, 20 (F. H. C. Birch), 24, 32 (Laura Lushing), 34; Robert Harding Picture Library p.36; Hutchison Library pp.44, 45; Mansell Collection p.43; Philip Parkhouse p.5; Gwyneth Windsor p.42.

The Publishers would like to thank the Ancient Art and Architecture Collection (Sinai Bible), and Impact/Mohamed Ansar (Reverend Joy Carrol) for the cover photographs.

Contents

1 Why the Bible is important

This unit tells you how important the Bible is for the Christian church.

The Bible is the most important book in the world for Christians. They read and study the Bible to increase their faith in Jesus. They say it is their **scripture**. That means it is their special religious book.

When an **Archbishop** of Canterbury is enthroned, he promises to keep and support the teachings of the Church of England. As he makes his oath, he kisses the Canterbury Gospels. They may have been handwritten 1,500 years ago in Italy.

In Britain people are given a Bible to hold if they are ever asked to give evidence in a law court. They are asked to say:

'I promise that the evidence I shall give shall be the truth, the whole truth and nothing but the truth, so help me God'.

Of course, people who belong to other religions can swear on their holy books instead of the Bible. Some Christians refuse to take oaths. Like people who have no religious beliefs, they can 'affirm'. This means they make the same promise without the Bible and without mentioning God.

Whenever Christians worship you are likely to find a Bible. It is read by Roman Catholic Christians in a service called the **Mass**. **Ministers** use it when they are giving talks called sermons during a service. In Anglican churches in England the Bible should always be open for people to read because of a royal order. It is put on a special stand called a lectern. This stand may be shaped like an eagle or a pelican with its wings spread out ready to fly.

The Bible Society

Mary Jones lived in the village of Llanfihangel near Abergynolwyn in North Wales. She heard the Bible read in **chapel** and wanted one of her own, but Welsh versions were

Court scene with someone taking the oath.

expensive and not many shops sold them. Mary saved up for six years, earning money from collecting firewood, patching clothes and selling the eggs her hens laid. Then she set out for the town of Bala where she had been told that a Bible could be bought. Mary walked barefoot and the journey of 25 miles took her a whole day. Someone gave her supper and a bed for the night. The next day she got her Bible and walked back home. Mr Charles, the man who gave Mary Jones her Bible, was so impressed by her that he decided to form a society which would arrange for the Bible to be printed in many languages and sold as cheaply as possible, so that everyone who wanted a copy could afford one. In 1804, two years after Mary Jones got her Bible, the British and Foreign Bible Society was formed. Today it is just called the Bible Society.

A lectern.

How much the scriptures mean to a believer

'How I love your law!
It is my study all day long.
Your commandment makes me wiser than my enemies,
for it is my possession for ever.
I have more insight than all my teachers,
for your instruction is my study:
I have more wisdom than those who are old,
because I have kept your precepts.
I do not set foot on any evil path
in my obedience to your word;
I do not swerve from your decrees,
for you have been my teacher.
How sweet is your promise to my palate,
sweeter on my tongue than honey!
From your precepts I learn wisdom;
therefore I hate every path of falsehood.
Your word is a lamp to my feet,
a light on my path;
I have bound myself by oath and solemn vow
to keep your just decrees.
I am cruelly afflicted;
Lord, revive me as you have promised.'
(*Psalm* 119:97–107)

NEW WORDS

Archbishop a senior bishop. The Archbishop of Canterbury is the leader of the Church of England. A bishop is the leading Anglican or Roman Catholic clergyman in a region

Chapel a place of worship. Some Christians use the word instead of church

Mass a service based on the last supper which Jesus ate with his disciples

Minister the title given to a clergy person in some churches, or anyone who conducts services

Scriptures special books from which people learn about their religion

2 What the Bible means to Christians

This unit shows that the Bible means a lot to individual Christians.

Every Christian agrees that the Bible is the most important Christian book. However, if you were to ask Christians why it is so important and what it means to them you would be given many different answers. Here are some.

'If we didn't have the Bible our understanding of God, as Christians, would be based on feelings and guesses instead of what the disciples taught about Jesus and what Jews hundreds of years earlier had learned about his God. It provides a guide in matters of faith. This doesn't mean that I take every word of the Bible literally. I don't. It is not a scientific or a history text book but it does contain the voice of God. In it God's spirit speaks to mine.'

'When I read the Bible it touches the deepest parts of my personality. On a good day I really experience the presence of God. Its words give me comfort, support and encouragement. Often they also challenge me and show me where I am falling short as a disciple of Jesus, but they never leave me in despair, feeling that I am a failure. If I am ready to let the Bible speak to me I am sure that I hear the voice of God. I believe that I do when I read other scriptures too, like the Qur'an, for example, but the Bible speaks in an even more special way to me. If it didn't I would not be a Christian. It is food for my spiritual life. I would starve without it.'

'The Bible is the most important book I own because it is my holy scripture. Although there is nearly always one book on the floor near my armchair at home I never put the Bible there because it contains God's word. I try to read the Bible every evening. After sitting quietly for a few minutes I slowly and thoughtfully read the Bible, asking God to show me something to learn. I often find that I specially notice a word, phrase or idea from the passage that I am reading. (It's almost like having the radio on in the background and something is said, or sung, and a word catches your ear.) I believe that God speaks to me in this way. Sometimes it is encouragement. At other times it is help in making a decision when I am not sure what to do. Or it may make me think about something that I am doing. Whatever my attention is drawn

An artificial leg being fitted for a leprosy patient in Nepal.

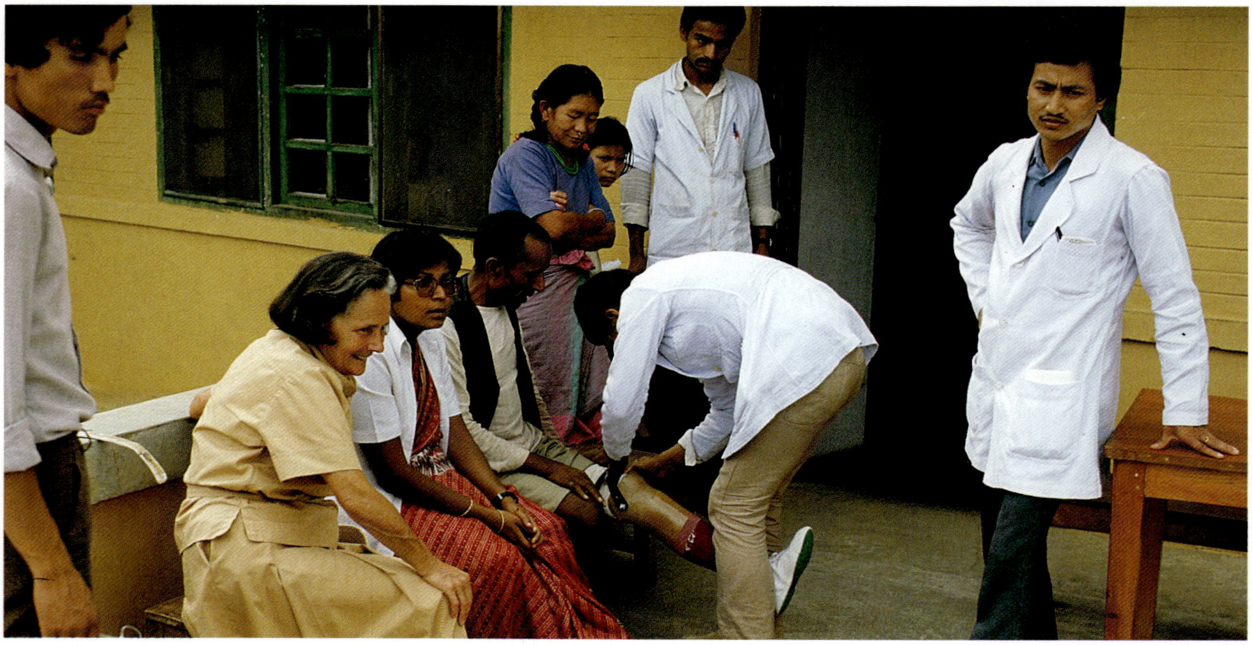

Most Christian homes are likely to own at least one Bible. Many Christians will read it every day.

> to, it always seems to be what I need at that moment. Although God speaks to me in different ways, the most important is through the Bible. I have found great encouragement and help from it in my daily life.'

> 'The Bible is alive, it speaks to me; it has feet, it runs after me; it has hands, it lays hold on me.'

All kinds of events change people's lives. One of the many who have been affected by the Bible was **Saint** Francis of Assisi (1182–1226). Francis came from a rich Italian family. When he was 20 he was put in prison for a year for taking part in a feud against a nearby city, but generally he lived a carefree life. Three years later he went on a pilgrimage to Rome and had a **vision** in which God told him to rebuild a fallen-down church in a village near Assisi. Francis sold his horse and some of the cloth his father traded in to buy materials for the church. His father disowned him! Francis wasn't quite sure what he should do with his life until, one day, 24 February 1208, he heard these words read while he was in church at worship:

> 'Proclaim "the Kingdom of Heaven is upon you". Heal the sick, raise the dead, cleanse lepers, drive out demons. You have received without cost, give without charge. Take no gold, silver or copper in your belts, no pack for the road, no second coat, no sandals, no stick.'

These words of Jesus from *Matthew's Gospel* 10:7–10 changed his life. He knew that these were the things that he must do. Francis gathered friends who shared his work. They became the Franciscan **friars**. They did not live in monasteries but travelled from place to place helping the poor and homeless, preaching to them, and sharing their way of life.

NEW WORDS

Friar 'brother' is its real meaning; member of a religious group which lives and works among the people rather than staying in a monastery

Saint in the Bible all Christians are called saints, but the Roman Catholic Church began to give the title to men and women whose Christian lives have been especially good; many are martyrs, people who were killed for their faith. (Abbreviated to St in this book)

Vision an inspiring thought or idea, but also an experience in which one sees a special person who gives one a message or a task to do

Faith and deeds must go together

'What good is it, my friends, for someone to say he has faith when his actions do nothing to show it? Can that faith save him? Suppose a fellow-Christian, whether man or woman, is in rags with not enough food for the day, and one of you says, "Goodbye, keep warm, and have a good meal," but does nothing to supply their bodily needs, what good is that? So with faith; if it does not lead to action, it is by itself a lifeless thing.' (*James* 2:14–17)

3 Jesus' holy scripture

This unit tells you about the scriptures that Jesus used.

Jesus was a Jew. He was born in a country which today is called Israel. Most of his life was spent in the north, in the region of Galilee, but he probably made many visits to the centre of Jewish worship, the Temple in Jerusalem.

Jesus' parents were devout Jews, so they took him to the Temple while he was still a baby to give thanks for him. (The story is told in *Luke* 2:22–40.) Each year they also made the journey from their home to Jerusalem, about 50 miles, to be at the Temple for a special festival, Passover. When Jesus was 12 he went with them (*Luke* 2:41–42). They probably walked, though women may have ridden on mules or donkeys.

It is only a little over 100 years ago that everyone began going to school in Britain, but education has always been important to Jews because they believed that everyone should be able to read their scriptures, the **Torah**.

As a child, Jesus would have learned to read and write the language of his scriptures, Hebrew, in a school at his local **synagogue**. He would have studied the Torah there. He would have heard and read the story of the way in which his ancestors had been delivered from Egypt, where they had been slaves. Although it had happened more than 1,000 years before he was born, Jesus and every other Jew remembered it at least three times each year at the festivals of Shavuot, which was also known as Pentecost, the anniversary of the giving of the Torah to the Jewish leader, Moses, at Mount Sinai; at Sukkot, when his family would live for eight days in shelters made of leaves and branches to remember the rough life of the refugees during their 40-year journey to Israel; and at Passover.

Passover was the greatest festival of all. It reminded Jews of the night when they left Egypt.

Jesus and the Passover festival

The last meal which Jesus ate with his friends was in Jerusalem to celebrate the same festival

In 70CE the Roman army destroyed the Jerusalem Temple. Only the Western Wall remains. This model is based on the research of archaeologists.

This Jewish boy is celebrating his religious coming of age, his bar mitzvah. Out of respect, he touches the Torah only with his prayer shawl, never his finger.

NEW WORDS

Prophet a person called by God to tell the Jews how to use the Torah

Sabbath Jewish day of rest when no humans or animals should be made to work

Sadducees religious group who believed there was no after-life for the soul following death

Synagogue place of Jewish worship

Torah the name Jews give to their whole scripture, as well to its most important section, the five books of Moses, *Genesis, Exodus, Leviticus, Numbers* and *Deuteronomy.* (Christians call it the Old Testament)

that he had attended as a twelve-year-old. They were all Jews, and Luke, a New Testament writer, suggests that they had sacrificed a lamb in the Temple like thousands of other Jews who were making the pilgrimage. They ate it together and thanked God for delivering the Jews from Egypt 1,200 years earlier. (See *Luke* 22:7–8.) Jesus would have read about the deliverance from Egypt in the Torah. In it God gave a promise:

> 'I am the Lord. I shall free you from your labours in Egypt and deliver you from slavery. I shall deliver you with outstretched arm and with mighty acts of judgement. I shall adopt you as my people, and I shall be your God. You will know that I the Lord am your God who frees you from your slavery in Egypt.' (*Exodus* 6:6–9)

The Torah didn't only tell Jews about their festivals; it also contained the story of the creation of the world, the calling of the Jews to serve God, and the commandments Jews should obey as God's people.

By the time of Jesus, many Jews also regarded other books to be scripture, the books of the **prophets**, such as *Jeremiah* and *Isaiah*, and the Writings, books like *Ruth* and *Psalms*. Jesus certainly did, but a group of Jews called **Sadducees** said that only the first five books were scripture.

The Sabbath

The Torah also instructed Jews how to keep their most important day of the week, the **Sabbath**. It is the seventh day and begins on Friday evening, when three stars can be seen clearly in the sky. It ends on Saturday when the three stars reappear. Every Sabbath they attend their local synagogue. Jesus worshipped regularly in the synagogue of his home town of Nazareth and was sometimes invited to be one of the readers of the scriptures.

Jerusalem

The writer recognizes that God is Lord of the whole earth.

'These are the words of the Lord:
The heavens are my throne and the earth is my footstool.
Where will you build a house for me,
where will my resting-place be?
These are all of my own making,
and all belong to me.
This is the word of the Lord.'

But Jerusalem is still special.

'Rejoice with Jerusalem and exult in her,
all you that love her;
share her joy with all your heart,
all you that mourned over her.
Then you may suck comfort from her and be satisfied,
taking with enjoyment her plentiful milk.'
(*Isaiah* 66:1–11)

4 How Jesus used his holy scripture

This unit show how Jesus interpreted the scripture differently from other Jews of his time.

Was Jesus a scribe?

Long before Jesus' time there were men who explained and interpreted the Torah. The Bible sometimes calls them '**scribes**'. Scribe means 'copyist' but they did much more than copy manuscripts of the scriptures in those days, long before the invention of printing. They also taught the meaning of the scripture. For example, the Torah says, 'An eye for an eye and a tooth for a tooth' (*Exodus* 21:24). The teachers said that this was not to be taken literally, as anyone will realize who reads from verses 22–27. (It is never wise to look at one sentence and ignore the rest!) This law was intended to stop endless blood feuds. Instead, the scribes said, an injured person should be fully compensated for:

1. the pain suffered,
2. doctor's fees,
3. loss of earnings,
4. personal humiliation, and
5. the actual damage.

Jesus may have been one of these teachers. They were later called **rabbis**, and this term is issued in *John's Gospel* by people when they are speaking to Jesus. Rabbis did not write down their teachings but passed them on to their **disciples** orally. However, rabbis were the pupils of other rabbis. Jesus never spoke of having a teacher, so it is impossible to be certain that he was a scribe. However, he behaved very much like one.

Jesus the teacher in the synagogue

In the New Testament St Luke described one service that Jesus attended in the synagogue. It was in his home town of Nazareth. Jesus read the scroll of the prophet Isaiah. This is what Luke wrote.

'Jesus came to Nazareth, where he had been brought up, and went to the synagogue on the Sabbath Day as he regularly did. He stood up to read the lesson and was handed the scroll of the prophet Isaiah. He opened the scroll and found the passage which says,

'"The Spirit of the Lord is upon me because he has anointed me; he has sent me to announce goods news to the poor, to proclaim release for prisoners and recovery of sight for the blind; to let the broken victims go free, to proclaim the year of the Lord's favour."

'He rolled up the scroll, gave it back to the attendant, and sat down; and all eyes in the synagogue were fixed on him. He began to address them: "Today," he said, "in your hearing, this scripture has come true."'

(*Luke* 4:16–21)

Israel at the time of Jesus.

When he had finished Jesus said: 'Today, in your hearing, this scripture has come true'. It annoyed some people so much that they wanted to kill him. They were probably shocked because Jesus seemed to claim to be the person that Isaiah was writing about.

In a section of *Matthew's Gospel*, known as the Sermon on the Mount, Jesus says things like:

> 'You have heard that our forefathers were told, "Do not commit murder; anyone who commits murder must be brought to justice." But what I tell you is this: Anyone who nurses anger against his brother must be brought to justice.'
>
> 'You have heard that they were told, "An eye for an eye and a tooth for a tooth." But what I say is this: Do not resist those who wrong you.'
>
> (*Matthew* 5:21–22; 38–39)

At the end of the Sermon on the Mount Matthew adds:

> 'When Jesus had finished this discourse the people were amazed at his teaching; unlike the scribes he taught with a note of authority.'
>
> (*Matthew* 7:28–29)

(You can read the whole Sermon on the Mount in *Matthew*, chapters 5, 6 and 7.)

NEW WORDS

Disciple the follower of a teacher such as Jesus or a rabbi

Messiah anointed one. Word used to describe the person promised by God to deliver his people, the Jews

Rabbi master. A religious teacher whose followers (disciples) learn from him and commit themselves to his way of life

Scribe a copyist of manuscripts, and also a Jewish teacher

Jesus seemed to be saying that he was greater than the scribes. Christians believe he made an even greater claim.

One day, after Jesus had been preaching in the Galilee region, near a place called Caesarea Philippi, Jesus asked his disciples, 'Who do people say that I am?' They told him of rumours that he was John the Baptist, his cousin, who had been executed by the Jewish ruler, Herod. Perhaps John had escaped being killed or even come back to life. Or he was Elijah, a prophet who did not die but was taken bodily into Heaven. He was said to return to earth now and again. Jesus' close friend Peter replied:

> 'You are the **Messiah**.' (*Mark* 8:29)

Jesus accepted Peter's words but then began to explain the kind of Messiah that he was. He said that he would have to endure suffering and even death. This was something unthinkable to his followers and to most other Jews.

The Beatitudes

Matthew's words of blessing to his followers.

'Blessed are the poor in spirit;
the kingdom of Heaven is theirs.
Blessed are the sorrowful;
they shall find consolation.
Blessed are the gentle;
they shall have the earth for their possession.
Blessed are those who hunger and thirst to see right prevail;
they shall be satisfied.
Blessed are those who show mercy;
mercy shall be shown to them.
Blessed are those whose hearts are pure;
they shall see God.
Blessed are the peacemakers;
they shall be called God's children.'

(*Matthew* 5: 1–9)

5 How Christians used the Jewish

This unit describes the way in which Jesus' followers said that the Jewish scriptures pointed to Jesus.

The Apostles

Jesus had many men and women disciples, but twelve men were chosen for a special task, to be **Apostles**. (The number twelve was important: it was symbolic of the twelve Jewish tribes.) The Apostles had spent all their time with Jesus from the beginning of his **ministry** until the end. One of them, Judas, betrayed Jesus and then committed suicide. Matthias was elected to take his place. As disciples these men had learned the message of Jesus. Now they were sent to pass it on to other Jews worldwide. They were instructed to tell them what they had seen. Most important of all, they were eye witnesses of Jesus' **resurrection**. They could say, 'Yes, it really did happen. We saw Jesus die and we saw him alive again!'

When the Apostles preached, they would share their own experiences of being with Jesus. They would also take sections of the Torah and show how they referred to Jesus. One of their favourite passages was from the scroll of the prophet Isaiah. They believed that it predicted the sufferings of Jesus. They would read these words:

> 'He was despised, shunned by all, painwracked and afflicted with disease; we despised him, we held him of no account, an object from which people turn away their eyes.
>
> 'Yet it was our afflictions he was bearing, our pain he endured, while we thought of him smitten by God, struck down by disease and misery. But he was pierced for our transgressions, crushed for our iniquities; the chastisement he bore restored us to health and by his wounds we are healed.
>
> 'We had all strayed like sheep, each of us going his own way, but the Lord laid on him the guilt of us all.
>
> 'He was maltreated, yet he was submissive and did not open his mouth; like a ewe that is dumb before the shearers, he did not open his mouth.
>
> 'He was arrested and sentenced and taken away, and who gave a thought for his fate – how he was cut off from the world of the living, stricken to death for my people's transgression?
>
> 'He was assigned a grave with the wicked, a burial place among felons, though he had done no violence, had spoken no word of treachery.'
>
> (*Isaiah* 53:3–9)

The Baptism of St Edwin painted by Ford Madox Brown.

Scriptures

These words from *Isaiah* were the most important verses which the **missionaries** used. They are quoted in the Christian books of the Bible far more than any other verses from the scriptures which Jesus knew.

The Apostles would point out similarities with the sufferings of Jesus and try to persuade their listeners that the prophet had been inspired to tell of the Messiah's coming to save his people.

One of the Christian books of the Bible tells the story of a Christian missionary called Philip explaining these words from *Isaiah* 53 to a court official from Ethiopia.

> 'The man had been in Jerusalem on a pilgrimage to the Temple and was now returning home. He was sitting in his carriage and reading aloud from the scroll of the prophet Isaiah. Philip felt inspired to speak to him and asked him whether he understood what he was reading. The official said,"How can I unless I have someone to guide me?" and invited Philip to join him.
>
> '"Please tell me," asked the official, "is the prophet speaking of himself or someone else?" Philip told him the good news about Jesus. When they came to a place where there was water, the Ethiopian asked to be baptized.'
>
> (The story is told in full in *Acts* 8:26–40)

The new covenant and the old

During the final meal which Jesus shared with his disciples, the Last Supper as Christians call it, Jesus said something which they must have found very difficult to understand. He took the cup of wine and passed it to them with the words:

> 'Drink from it, all of you. For this is my blood, the blood of the **covenant**, shed for many for the forgiveness of sins.' (*Matthew* 26:27–28)

At Mount Sinai God had made a covenant in which he chose the Jews to be his people. He said that he would meet their needs and they must obey the Torah. Now Jesus was speaking of a new relationship based on faith in him, not on keeping the Torah. It would be open to all those who believed in him. It replaced the old covenant. Eventually Christians began to regard the Jewish scriptures as the 'books of the old covenant'. The Latin word for 'covenant' is 'testamentum', so the first part of the Bible which Christians use now came to be called the Old Testament. The part which focuses on Jesus is called the New Testament.

NEW WORDS

Apostle an eye witness of Jesus' ministry, sent to preach about him to other people

Covenant an agreement between God and his people. They promise to serve him; he promises to protect them

Ministry Jesus' work of preaching, teaching and helping the needy

Missionary someone who tries to make other people share his or her beliefs

Resurrection return to life after dying

Some words of hope about the Messianic age

'See, I am creating new heavens and a new earth! The past will no more be remembered, nor will it ever come to mind. Rejoice and be forever filled with delight at what I create; for I am creating Jerusalem as a delight and her people as a joy; I shall take delight in Jerusalem and rejoice in my people; the sound of weeping, the cry of distress will be heard in her no more. No child there will ever again die in infancy, no old man fail to live out his span of life. He who dies at a hundred is just a youth, and if he does not attain a hundred he is thought accursed!'

(*Isaiah* 65:17–20)

6 St Paul

This unit tells you about the man who wrote more New Testament books than anyone else. (Most of them were letters.)

If you turn to the contents page of a Bible you will find that about four-fifths of it was inherited from Judaism. This is the Old Testament. The New Testament happened almost by accident. Most of it was written by a man called Paul.

St Paul is the most important person (after Jesus, of course) in the story of the New Testament. Much is known about his life; in fact, he may be the best known Roman citizen in history, apart from some of the emperors. He was born in the important city of Tarsus.

Saul was the name by which Paul was first known. His parents probably named him after the first Jewish king. His family were at least fairly wealthy because they were Roman citizens, and that meant that they had to own property, unless they were actually born in Rome. As a Roman citizen, Saul had a Roman name. It was Paulus (Paul in English). Paul's trade was sail and tent-making. This wasn't surprising, as Tarsus was a large port and many travellers going inland from it would use tents. His father would have taught him. Jews usually went into the family business.

Paul was educated in Greek, the civilized language of the Roman world, but he also is said to have studied the Torah in Jerusalem as the disciple of Rabbi Gamaliel, one of the greatest teachers of his time (*Acts* 22:3).

Paul the Pharisee

Pharisees were men who dedicated their lives to understanding the Torah. They kept its teachings as faithfully as they could, and encouraged others to live according to its instructions. They told the people of their own day how they should keep the Torah, as the prophets of earlier times had done.

Jesus was probably a Pharisee. Paul certainly was. In one of his letters he wrote that he was a Pharisee (*Philippians* 3:5).

Paul, persecutor of the church

The followers of Jesus soon began to call themselves the **ecclesia**. This is a Greek word meaning members of a city which had been given the right to rule itself. In Greek versions of the Old Testament it also referred to the nation of Israel. In English the word used to translate ecclesia is **church**. It came to be used of special buildings, but it really means the people who worship in them, those who have been called by God to be the people of God.

Paul believed that people who claimed that Jesus was the Messiah were utterly wrong. He felt that they threatened all that the Torah

The Roman world which St Paul knew. Notice the important trading position of Tarsus.

stood for. He was willing to see them punished, even killed. He volunteered to hunt them down. Paul's mission as a persecutor took him to Damascus, a city in Syria about 140 miles north of Jerusalem (only 60 miles from Galilee, where most Christians lived). Luke, who was later a companion of Paul, described what happened to Paul as he approached the city in the *Acts of the Apostles*. He wrote:

> 'While he (Paul) was still on the road and nearing Damascus, suddenly a light from the sky flashed all around him. He fell to the ground and heard a voice saying to him, "Saul, Saul, why are you persecuting me?" "Tell me Lord," he said, "who you are." The voice answered, "I am Jesus, whom you are persecuting. But now, get up and go into the city, and you will be told what you have to do."' (*Acts* 9:3–7)

Paul, who had been blinded by the light, was taken to the house of a disciple named Ananias, where he regained his sight after three days and was baptized.

Paul was the most important convert to the young church. He knew his Torah. He would be able to argue with those who could not believe that Jesus was the Messiah. He could tell them that he had once shared their views and explain why he had changed his mind. But he knew too little about Jesus' life and teachings to be of much use. He had to be retrained. This took some years. One day the church in Jerusalem decided to send a disciple called Barnabas to the city of Antioch in Syria and told him to take Paul. He went to Tarsus to find him; perhaps Paul was back home waiting for something to happen. Now his new career as a Christian missionary began.

NEW WORDS

Church a Christian community, or the building which they use

Ecclesia Greek word for church

Paul often used the example of Jesus to encourage Christians

'If then our common life in Christ yields anything to stir the heart, any consolation of love, any participation in the Spirit, any warmth of affection or compassion, fill up my cup of happiness by thinking and feeling alike, with the same love for one another and a common attitude of mind. Leave no room for selfish ambition and vanity, but humbly reckon others better than yourselves. Look to each other's interests and not merely to your own. Take to heart among yourselves what you find in Christ Jesus: "He was in the form of God; yet he laid no claim to equality with God, but made himself nothing, assuming the form of a slave. Bearing the human likeness, sharing the human lot, he humbled himself, and was obedient, even to the point of death, death on a cross!

(*Philippians* 2:1–8)

Do you know?

The nickname 'Christians' was first used in Antioch to describe the disciples of Jesus. It comes from 'Christos', the Greek word for 'Messiah', and means 'those who say the Messiah has come' (*Acts* 11:26).

London's great cathedral is dedicated to the missionary Apostle St Paul.

7 St Peter

This unit is about St Peter, one of the most important people behind the New Testament.

St Peter is the best known of the Apostles. He was one of the first men that Jesus asked to follow him. Peter was a fisherman on the lake of Galilee. Jesus may have known Peter for many years before he called him to become a disciple. When Jesus was arrested, Peter lost his nerve and said that he didn't even know him, but he plucked up enough courage to follow Jesus to the place where he was tried, only to be overcome by fear again. A few weeks later, however, he was telling the people of Jerusalem that the person they had seen executed was the Messiah and that he was alive.

The calling of St Peter, disciple of John the Baptist

'The next day again, John was standing with two of his disciples, when Jesus passed by. John looked towards him and said, "There is the Lamb of God!" One of the two disciples who followed Jesus after hearing what John the Baptist said was Andrew, Simon Peter's brother. The first thing he did was to find his brother Simon and say to him, "We have found the Messiah" (which is the Hebrew for Christ). He brought Simon to Jesus, who looked at him and said, "You are Simon son of John; you shall be called Cephas" (that is, Peter, 'the Rock').' (*John* 1:35–42)

Although some of the first visitors to the child Jesus, the **Magi**, had been non-Jews, most of his ministry had been only to his own people. All his men and women followers were Jews. Only Jews were looking for a Messiah. It seemed quite natural, therefore, that Peter and the rest of the Apostles should limit their preaching to Jews. If it were not for one very important event in Peter's life, 'Christianity' might have remained a minor movement within the Jewish religion. Only Jews might have been allowed to be Christians.

Two things happened to change the course of Christian history.

Peter's dream

The first incident is told in *Acts* in Peter's own words.

> 'I was at prayer in the city of Joppa', he said, 'and while in a trance I had a vision: I saw something coming down that looked like a great sheet of sailcloth, slung by the four corners and lowered from heaven until it reached me. I looked intently to make out what was in it and I saw four-footed beasts, wild animals, reptiles and birds. Then I heard a voice saying to me, "Get up, Peter kill and eat." But I said, "No, Lord! Nothing **profane** has ever entered my mouth." A voice from heaven came a second time: "It is not for you to call profane what God counts clean." This happened three times, and then they were all drawn up again into heaven. At that very moment three men who had been sent to me from Caesarea arrived at the house where I was staying; and the Spirit told me to go with them. My six companions came here with me

St Peter's Cathedral in Rome is the central church of Roman Catholic Christianity. St Peter may be buried beneath it.

Joppa (Jaffa) harbour today.

> and we went into the man's house. He told us how he had seen an angel standing in his house who had said, "Send to Joppa for Peter. He will speak words that will bring salvation to you and to all your household." Hardly had I begun speaking, when the Holy Spirit came upon them just as it had at the beginning, and I recalled what the Lord had said: "John baptized with water, but you will be baptized with the Holy Spirit." God gave them no less a gift than he gave us when we came to believe in the Lord Jesus. How could I stand in God's way?' (*Acts* 11:5–16)

This convinced Peter that anyone of any race could become a Christian.

St Paul and St Barnabas preach to non-Jews

The second event happened when St Paul and Barnabas were preaching and some non-Jews were present. They became believers and told others who also wanted to become Christians. What should happen to these converts? Should they be baptized? Should they become Jews first by accepting the Torah and then be baptized? Eventually, the leaders of the church met in Jerusalem. Paul and Barnabas gave their account of what had happened. Peter proposed that baptism should be the only requirement for membership of the church. James, brother of Jesus and chairman of the discussion, laid down a few rules so that Jewish Christians would not be caused distress.

These were:

- not to eat food offered to idols (the left-overs were sold cheaply in the market. This was the only meat some people could afford);
- not to be sexually immoral;
- not to eat meat containing blood (Jews drained off as much of the blood as they could);
- not to eat meat killed by strangling (it would still contain blood).

(The list is given in *Acts* 15:19–21.)

From now on, all of the Apostles were free to baptize anyone who said that they believed in Jesus as their Lord. Paul never gave up preaching to members of his Jewish community, but most of his work, for the rest of his life, was to the general public of the Roman Empire.

NEW WORDS

Magi the visitors from the East who came to see the child Jesus. It is not clear that they were three, wise, or even men, so it is safer to use 'Magi' (see *Matthew*, chapter 2)

Profane irreverent, not sacred; in this case, food which was forbidden in the Torah (not kosher; that is, not fit to be eaten according to the Torah)

The Council of Jerusalem letter to all churches

'From the apostles and elders to our brothers of gentile origin in Antioch, Syria, and Cilicia. Greetings! We are sending Judas and Silas, who will, by word of mouth, confirm what is written in this letter. It is the decision of the Holy Spirit, and our decision, to lay no further burden upon you beyond these essentials: you are to abstain from meat that has been offered to idols, from blood, from anything that has been strangled, and from fornication.'

(*Acts* 15:23, 27–29)

8 St Paul: the traveller and writer

This unit describes some of St Paul's adventures, and the first New Testament book.

A sail-maker needs to know how boats work and must feel happy on the water. St Paul must have done, because he made at least four sea journeys, though the last was not from choice. His liking for the sea was something unusual. Romans preferred to keep land in sight if they could. They would rather travel by road than by boat.

St Paul was a missionary. The reason for his journeys was simple. He wanted to persuade people to become disciples of Jesus, the Lord, as he called him, to whom he had given his life in Damascus.

St Paul went to towns which were important for one reason or another. Most were in places where main roads met, or were market centres. Others, like Ephesus, were famous for religious reasons. St Paul worked to a plan.

Where to find out about Paul

The *Acts of the Apostles* is the book of the Bible that tells most about him. It was written by a man called Luke, who was Paul's companion on many journeys. In this unit we will look at only a few stories from Paul's life, but there are suggestions of others that you can read for yourself at the end of Unit 9.

The eastern part of the Roman Empire, showing most of the places St Paul visited.

Paul's first journey had been with Barnabas to Antioch and Cyprus and some Turkish cities. On the second journey they returned to some of these places to see how the young churches were managing. On the way they met one of the converts, Timothy, and invited him to be their companion. Then they went into Greece and came to Philippi. It was rather like the Roman cities of York, Gloucester, Exeter or Caerwent in Britain: large and well planned. It was a 'colonia', which was somewhere for ex-legionaries of the Roman army to settle on their retirement. Luke describes a healing there.

> 'On our way to the place of prayer, we met a slave girl who was possessed by a spirit of divination and made large profits for her owners by telling fortunes. She followed Paul and the rest of us, shouting, "These are men of the Most High God, and are declaring to you a way of salvation." She did this day after day, until, in exasperation, Paul rounded on the spirit. "I command you in the name of Jesus Christ to come out of her," he said, and it came out instantly.' (*Acts* 16:16–18)

The owners of the girl were not pleased. Their income had gone with her power to tell fortunes. They hauled Paul and a companion, Silas, to the magistrates, who had them whipped for making a disturbance. They were then put in prison. That night there was an earthquake. The prison doors collapsed. The gaoler drew his sword to commit suicide. He thought that Paul and Silas had escaped. If they had, he would be executed, so he might as well do the honourable thing. Paul shouted out that they had not run away, so there was no need for him to harm himself. The gaoler took them to his home, where he and his family became Christians.

Next morning, the magistrates ordered the release of Paul and Silas. But Paul refused to go. 'We are Roman citizens,' he said. 'They gave us a public flogging and threw us into prison without trial. Are they now going to smuggle us out by stealth? No indeed! Let

St Paul may have passed the Library of Celsius at Ephesus on his journey to Rome as a captive.

them come in person and escort us out.' When the magistrates heard that they were Roman citizens they were afraid that they would be punished for their injustice and politely asked Paul and Silas to leave the city. Paul and Silas, however, insisted on going to the house of Lydia, the convert with whom they had been staying. Only when they had spoken words of encouragement to the Christians did they depart.

Thessalonica: Paul's first letters

Paul and Silas preached in Thessalonica's synagogue for three Sabbaths. They quoted the Torah in an attempt to convince the congregation that Jesus was the Messiah. Some men and influential women became Christians but others did not. There were riots. Paul and Silas decided to leave for Athens and Corinth. Some time later, Timothy returned to Thessalonica to see how the Christians were getting on. When Paul heard Timothy's report he decided to write to the church. It is possible to make a good guess at what Timothy said by reading *1 Thessalonians*. Things were pretty good. The Christians were caring for one another and standing firm. But they were not sure what Paul had meant when he told them that Jesus would return to complete his work and rule as Lord. As they waited for this return they also worried about those who had died before it happened. Paul assured them that when the Lord came the Christian dead would rise first and then living Christians would join them

> 'caught up in clouds to meet the Lord in the air'
> (*I Thessalonians* 4:17)

This letter was misunderstood. When it was read to the congregation in Thessalonica, some members were so fascinated by the idea of Jesus' coming that they gave up their jobs so they could prepare for it spiritually. Paul had to remind them that when he and his companions had been with them they had worked at their various occupations so as not to be a burden on the church. He also reminded them of his rule:

> 'anyone who will not work shall not eat'
> (*2 Thessalonians* 3:10)

He said they were not religious, just lazy!

These two letters seem to have been Paul's first ones, and the first books of the New Testament. They were probably written from Corinth in 50CE, during his eighteen-month-long stay there.

St Paul encourages Christians to trust in Jesus

'We wish you not to remain in ignorance, friends, about those who sleep in death; you should not grieve like the rest of mankind, who have no hope. We believe that Jesus died and rose again; so too will God bring those who died as Christians to be with Jesus.

'This we tell you as a word from the Lord: those of us who are still alive when the Lord comes will have no advantage over those who have died; when the command is given, when the archangel's voice is heard, when God's trumpet sounds, then the Lord himself will descend from heaven; first the Christian dead will rise, then we who are still alive shall join them, caught up in clouds to meet the Lord in the air. Thus we shall always be with the Lord. Console one another, then, with these words.'

(*1 Thessalonians* 3:13–18)

9 St Paul's letters from prison

This unit is about some of the letters which St Paul wrote from prison.

Why were some of Paul's letters preserved?

We don't keep every greetings card and letter that we receive. The Christians at Corinth didn't save all the letters they got from Paul. There are clues to suggest that he wrote at least four to them. Why did any survive? Here are some reasons.

First, as St Paul's fame grew churches might have wanted to keep the letters which he had sent them. Secondly, some of the letters contained important advice and teaching.

Thirdly, the return of the Lord, which St Paul sometimes wrote about, showed no signs of happening. It seemed sensible to keep the letters which he had sent and perhaps start collecting ones he had sent to other churches.

There might be at least one other reason. St Paul wrote four **epistles**, or letters, in which he says he is in gaol: *Colossians*, *Ephesians*, *Philemon* and *Philippians*. The only long stay in prison that Luke mentions is in Rome. Most people think that they were written from there. Paul does, however, refer to fighting with wild beasts at Ephesus (*1 Corinthians* 15:32). Perhaps some of these letters were written in a cell in Ephesus. It doesn't matter too much. It is always what letters say that is important; but if imprisonment carried with it the possibility of execution, by being thrown to the lions as public entertainment in an arena, or being beheaded, it is understandable that a church would want to keep a letter from Paul.

The theatre at Ephesus where St Paul is said to have fought with wild beasts (I Corinthians 15:32).

Like many Jews of his day, St Paul believed in the Devil and the power of evil. (Many Christians still share his belief.) At the close of one of his letters from prison he instructed the Christians to be armed against evil.

> 'Stand fast, I say. Fasten on the belt of truth; for a breastplate put on integrity; let the shoes on your feet be the gospel of peace, to give you firm footing; and with all these take up the great shield of faith, with which you will be able to quench all the burning arrows of the evil one. Accept salvation as your helmet, and the sword which the Spirit gives you, the word of God.'
> (*Ephesians* 6:14–17)

Paul's shortest letter

During his stay in prison, Paul found himself sharing a cell with a young runaway slave, Onesimus. He had been captured and was waiting to be returned to his owner. It turned out that Onesimus' master, Philemon, was a Christian whom Paul knew well. During the anxious days of his imprisonment the slave became a Christian, but that might not save his skin when he was handed back to his owner. It would be unlawful for Philemon to kill Onesimus but he could whip him, make his life a misery, and sell him to someone who would treat him even more cruelly. Paul decided to appeal to Philemon's better nature. He wrote his letter in the style of Roman letters. He begins:

> 'From Paul, a prisoner of Christ Jesus, and our colleague Timothy, to Philemon, Apphia [his wife, perhaps?], and Archippus [maybe his son?]....'

Instead of the word which usually followed, 'greetings', Paul went on,

> 'Grace to you and peace from God our Father and the Lord Jesus Christ.'

After a few friendly words, Paul gets to the point.

> 'Although in Christ I might feel free to dictate where your duty lies, yet, because of that same love, I would rather appeal to you. Ambassador as I am of Christ Jesus, and now his prisoner, I, Paul, appeal to you about my child, whose father I have become in this prison. I mean Onesimus.'

He ended the letter by sending greetings from those who were with him. Onesimus may have robbed his owner before running away. The slave would have nothing of his own that he could give to make up the loss so Paul asks Philemon to put it down to his account, and adds his signature as an extra assurance of his promise to pay. It made it legally binding. (Probably Paul's letters were actually dictated to someone else. Such a person was called an **amanuensis**.) Finally, Paul says that he hopes to visit Philemon shortly:

> 'Have a room ready for me, for I hope through the prayers of you all to be restored to you.'

No one knows whether Paul was released and managed to stay with Philemon, his family and Onesimus. Perhaps even if Paul was not released the story had a happy ending. The leader of the church in Ephesus about 50 years later was called Onesimus. It might have been the same man. It is impossible to be sure, but it is an interesting coincidence.

Where to find out more about Paul

In the *Second Letter to the Corinthians* Paul criticizes those who are proud of the things they do for Jesus. He says he could boast if he wanted to, and gives a list of his sufferings. These are just some of them.

> 'Five times the Jews have given me the 39 strokes; three times I have been beaten with rods; once I was stoned; three times I have been ship-wrecked, and for 24 hours I was adrift in the open sea.' (*2 Corinthians* 11:24–27).

Not all of these events are mentioned in *Acts*. Luke only told the things which he thought it was most important for people to know about. Some other events are mentioned in *Acts* 19:23–41, 20:7–12 (a story which shows that Paul's preaching could send people to sleep), and 23:1–10.

NEW WORDS

Amanuensis a person who writes a letter dictated by someone else

Epistle sometimes Bibles list the epistles of Paul in their contents. Epistle is just another word meaning letter

Why Paul may have been imprisoned in Ephesus

'About then the Christian movement gave rise to a serious disturbance. There was a...silversmith who made silver shrines of Artemis, and provided considerable employment for the craftsmen. He called a meeting of them and of the workers in allied trades, and said: "As you men know, our prosperity depends on this industry. But this fellow Paul...has perverted crowds of people with his propaganda, not only at Ephesus but also in practically the whole of the province of Asia; he tells them that gods made by human hands are not gods at all. There is danger for us here: it is not only that our line of business will be discredited, but also that the sanctuary of the great goddess Artemis will cease to command respect." On hearing this, they were enraged, and began to shout "Great is Artemis of the Ephesians!" The whole city was in an uproar.' (*Acts* 19:23–29)

10 St Paul's great wish

This unit is about St Paul's wish to visit Rome and the letter which he sent to its Christians.

The biggest city in the Roman world in St Paul's time was Rome. About two million people lived there. It was a place that most people longed to visit. St Paul certainly did. He actually wrote a letter to the Christians of Rome introducing himself and saying that he hoped that he would meet them one day. Usually he only wrote to towns which he had already visited.

Paul's letter to the Roman Christians

Many members of the church in Rome were converts from Judaism. It seems that they thought that their new religion was about keeping rules. Paul reminded them of a verse in their scriptures which the prophet Habbakuk had written: 'The just shall live by faith' (*Habbakuk* 2:4). He told them that no one could please God simply by following a code of laws. He reminded them of one of the greatest men in their history, Abraham. He had put his trust in God. At God's command Abraham had left his home country and family and travelled thousand of miles to Israel, trusting that God would guide him. That is why God chose him to become a leader and the father of the nation of Israel. (You can read the story of Abraham in *Genesis*:12.)

Paul also used the word **grace**. It means God's undeserved love, something that cannot be earned by good deeds. It is a love which God gives because God is loving. Paul often said that he didn't deserve it. He had even persecuted Christians, but God was forgiving. Paul said that grace was not just a love which gives someone a warm and friendly feeling towards others. Grace is a love which gives strength to be good and to overcome temptation. God's love was shown most completely in Jesus who trusted in God, his father, and obeyed him even to the point of death. God raised him to life. Paul said:

> 'All have sinned, and been deprived of God's glory; and all are justified by God's free grace alone, through his act of liberation in the person of the Christ, Jesus.' (*Romans* 3:23)

St Paul taught that the story of Adam and Eve in the Jewish Scriptures was not just about one couple. Their disobedience had affected everyone. It was as if they had all caught Adam's disease. Only Jesus' obedience had been able to put things right. He was God's remedy for the disease of **sin**. Anyone who put their trust in Jesus would be saved.

The meaning of baptism

St Paul had also heard that there were other Christians who believed they could do what they liked so long as they believed in Jesus. He was as severe on them as on those who emphasized rules rather than faith:

> 'Have you forgotten that when we were baptized into union with Christ Jesus we were baptized into his death?' (*Romans* 6:3)

Baptism was not a permit to do what they liked. If they followed Jesus they must live like

Clifford's Tower in York is a reminder of the Jewish massacre of 1190.

Yad Vashem in Jerusalem is a memorial to the six million Jews who died in the Holocaust. The names of the death camps are marked in Roman script and Hebrew on the floor of the hall.

him. They must be God's slaves, not doing what they wanted when they knew it was wrong and that it would hurt other people.

Does God still care for the Jews?

This was a question which worried Jews who had become Christians in Paul's time. They would have brothers, sisters, parents and friends who could not bring themselves to believe that Jesus was the Messiah. Paul was preaching the belief that salvation depended upon faith in Jesus. Paul's answer was that Christians certainly ought not to regard Jews as enemies. God had revealed himself to the world through Jews like Abraham, Moses, Jesus and Paul. If all Jews had followed Jesus immediately, the message might never have been preached to the **Gentiles**, and they would not have become Christian. Those who rejected Jesus actually gave his non-Jewish readers their chance!

Paul wrote:

> 'Through a false step on their part salvation has come to the Gentiles.' (*Romans* 11:11)

Even if it seemed, from a Christian point of view, that the Jews might have turned their backs on God, by not accepting Jesus as their Messiah, nevertheless, God had not rejected his people.

Like Jesus, Paul was a Jew. He never stopped worshipping in the Temple when he was in Jerusalem and in synagogues wherever he was on the Sabbath. He always believed that his people remained God's people. He would have had no time for some Christians who persecuted Jews in later centuries. In Britain in 1190 the Jews of York were massacred. In 1290 the last Jews in Britain were expelled. (Jews were allowed to return in the time of Oliver Cromwell in 1657.) During the war of 1939–45, six million Jews were murdered. Sometimes Christians who have taken part in these persecutions claimed that they were punishing the Jews for killing Jesus!

The *Letter to the Romans* ended with Paul saying that he intended to visit Rome on his way to Spain (15:28). He added greetings to over 20 Christian friends who were now in Rome. It was obviously the place for missionaries to head for.

NEW WORDS

Gentiles non-Jews

Grace God's undeserved powerful love

Sin disobeying God

A possible source of anti-semitism in modern times

A passage from Martin Luther's pamphlet *Concerning the Jews and their Lies*: 'Their synagogues or churches should be set on fire and whatever does not burn should be covered or spread over with dirt so that no one may ever be able to see a cinder or stone of it. Their homes should likewise be destroyed. Their rabbis must be forbidden under threat of death to teach any more. All their cash and valuables of gold and silver ought to be taken from them and put aside for safe-keeping...if this advice of mine does not suit you, then find a better one so that you and we may all be free of this insufferable devilish burden – the Jews.'

11 St Peter and St Paul in Rome

This unit suggests why the *Acts of the Apostles* was written.

The *Acts of the Apostles*

St Paul got to Rome eventually, but not in the way he planned! He returned to Jerusalem from his third missionary journey. To show critics that he had not turned from his Jewish tradition, he joined some friends in a fast. At the end of it they went to the Temple to fulfil a vow. Some Jews thought that Paul had taken Gentiles into a part of the Temple from which they were banned. A riot broke out. Paul was arrested. He claimed his right as a Roman citizen to be tried in Rome in front of the Emperor. So he was shipped off to Rome. The voyage was a disaster. (Luke describes it in *Acts:* 27.) There was a storm, during which Paul remained calm and told the crew and the soldiers not to panic. They were shipwrecked on the island of Malta. At last they reached Rome. His great wish had come true – and at the Emperor's expense! The Christians were waiting for him.

Ruins of the Roman Forum in Rome. Look for the Arch of Emperor Titus and the Colosseum.

How did Christianity reach Rome?

Nobody knows. The best guess may be that it was first taken by Christian business people, such as a couple called Aquila and Priscilla, tent-makers. In Corinth Paul had stayed with them (*Acts* 18:2). They were Jewish converts who had been living in Rome. In his greetings at the end of his letter to Rome they are mentioned again.

There is also a suggestion that St Peter took Christianity to Rome. After the gathering of Christians in Jerusalem to discuss the Gentile conversion question (see page 17) he is not mentioned in the *Acts of the Apostles*. Perhaps St Peter was given the great task of establishing a Christian community in Rome. It is possible, of course, that there were already Christians in Rome, and that they visited Jerusalem for one of the Jewish festivals, met Peter, and persuaded him to go to Rome.

St Peter, first bishop of Rome

The church in Rome has kept a list of its bishops from the beginning of its existence. Peter is named as the first. It is said that he was its leader for 25 years. Sometimes it has been pointed out that the Apostles did not settle in any single place. They travelled around, as St Paul did. They were the only witnesses to the whole ministry of Jesus, so they had to share what they knew and had seen as widely as possible. Perhaps Peter didn't intend to stay in Rome when he went there but found so much to do that he remained there. Or, as he grew older, he was unable to travel. Roman Catholics certainly believe that St Peter was the first **Pope**.

Church leaders, bishops, were sometimes called father, or Pope. The title died out elsewhere in the Christian world but the bishop of Rome kept using it. Eventually, the Roman Pope became leader of the whole Catholic church, partly because he was the successor of Peter but also because Rome was the capital of the Empire.

Why was the *Acts of the Apostles* written?

The main characters in the book are Peter and Paul. The story of Peter ends after the meeting in Jerusalem (see page 17). The story of Paul ends with him as a prisoner in Rome under house arrest. If Peter had gone to Rome from Jerusalem there would be no need for Luke, the author of *Acts*, to tell any more of his story. He could tell it himself. The Roman Christians would know the story of Paul after he had reached Rome. Many episodes which Luke tells are about Peter and especially Paul being unjustly thrown into prison. It could be that Luke wrote his book to show that the two great Christians were not the criminals which some people were calling them. Later on, probably, he wrote his other book, the *Gospel of Luke*, partly to show that Jesus was an innocent person, too.

Acts is not the history of the early church. Most of the Apostles are not mentioned at all: St Thomas, for example. He may have reached India just after the Romans began to conquer Britain or St Peter went to Rome.

NEW WORD

Pope the leader of Roman Catholic Christians

Did Paul ever get to Spain?

The last sentence of *Acts* describes St Paul's fairly comfortable imprisonment in Rome:

> 'He stayed there two full years at his own expense, with a welcome for all who came to him; he proclaimed the kingdom of God and taught the facts about the Lord Jesus quite openly and without hindrance.' (28:30–31)

Traditions say that at the end of that time he was released and completed his planned visit to Spain. Clement, a bishop of Rome, wrote to the Christians in Corinth in about 95CE, saying that Paul did reach Spain.

The deaths of Peter and Paul

Clement, bishop of Rome, wrote in 96CE 'Through jealousy and envy the greatest and most righteous pillars (of the Church) were persecuted, and contended unto death. Let us set before our eyes the good (i.e. heroic) Apostles: Peter, who through unrighteous jealousy endured many labours, and so having borne witness went to his due place of glory. Through jealousy and strife Paul displayed the prize of endurance; seven times in bonds, driven into exile, stoned, appearing as a herald in both the East and the West he won noble fame for his faith; he taught righteousness to the whole world.'

12 The deaths of Peter and Paul

This unit tells of a persecution in Rome which may have made Christians decide to write more books.

In the year 64CE the Emperor Nero set fire to part of the city of Rome because he wanted to expand the grounds of his palace. He destroyed the houses which stood in his way. At least that is what the rumours said. To stop these tales leading to riots Nero had to find a scapegoat, someone to blame. He chose the Christians. This is the description of what he did to them. It was written by a Roman historian named Tacitus.

> 'All the gifts which the emperor made to the people and to the gods could not get rid of the rumour that the fire had been caused by the emperor's orders. Nero, therefore, decided to set up the Christians, who were hated by the general population. Christ, from whom they take their name, suffered execution during the reign of Tiberius at the hands of a procurator, Pontius Pilate. The deadly superstition, checked for a moment, broke out again – not only in Judaea, where the evil began, but also in the city of Rome to which shameful things come from all over the world. All who confessed that they were Christians were arrested first; they informed on others. Large numbers were arrested not for arson so much as for hatred of the human race. They were executed and mocked in the process. Animal skins were tied to their bodies and then dogs were set on them. They were nailed to crosses or burned. Christians were used as human torches to light up Nero's gardens which were opened to the public at night. Eventually, a feeling of pity developed for the criminals even though they deserved their punishment. It seemed that they were not being destroyed for the public good but to satisfy one man's enjoyment of cruelty.'
>
> (Written about 112CE. Tacitus was six years old in 64CE. Author's paraphrase.)

Rumours about Christians

Christians were thought to be wicked. It was rumoured that they talked about drinking blood and eating flesh in one of their secret rituals! Like Jews, they refused to worship the Emperor. Perhaps they were plotting against him. They talked of the end of the world. They might be using their prayers to make it happen; that would explain the flooding of Rome's river, the Tiber, and why grain ships from Egypt sank (like the one Paul was on!). Rumours always seem to grow up around new

The Colosseum, Rome, where human beings were forced to fight each other or wild beasts to the death.

The catacombs are underground caves and quarries beneath Rome and other cities. Christians sheltered in them and used them as cemeteries. One Christian painted pictures of St Peter and St Paul on a wall.

religious movements, in the Roman world and today.

Christian tradition teaches that Paul was beheaded, as a Roman citizen should be, and Peter was crucified on the same day. Nero's persecution took place only in Rome, but it shattered the whole Christian world. The first shock to the followers of Jesus had been Jesus' own execution. Now his two most famous Apostles were dead.

What should replace the Apostles?

James the Apostle had been beheaded in 44CE (*Acts* 12:2) but nothing certain is known about the deaths of the other Apostles. However, by now they must have been approaching old age. The return of Jesus, which his followers had hoped for, had not happened. Christians must have been wondering what to do when there were no longer any Apostles to give their testimonies to Jesus' ministry. The Apostles had passed on the story to their converts and each church had members who knew it well, but could their word always be trusted? They might forget, though people in the ancient world, like many in the east today, had minds which were trained as well as any actor's to remember large quantities of material. To learn the *Acts of the Apostles* by heart wouldn't have presented much of a challenge!

A solution

There were already arguments about some of Jesus' teachings, as Paul's letters show. It might be convenient for those who were rich to forget the things Jesus said about caring for the poor. Those who would like to fight the Romans might neglect Jesus' teachings that his followers should be peacemakers. The solution seems to have been to write everything down. Mark, a companion of Peter and Paul in Rome, was asked to do it. About 60 years later a bishop wrote:

> 'Mark, having been the interpreter of Peter, wrote accurately, though not in order, all that he recalled of what was said or done by the Lord. Mark neither heard the Lord, nor was a follower of his, but, at a later date, he was a companion of Peter, who used to adapt them to the needs of the moment. So Mark did nothing wrong in writing down things as he recalled them. He kept a single aim in view; not to omit anything that he had heard, and not to put down anything that was false.'
>
> (Papias, Bishop of Hierapolis, about 130CE)

Peter and Paul

Dionysius, bishop of the Corinthians, wrote to the Romans in about 170CE.

'In these ways you also, by such an admonition, have united the planting that came from Peter and Paul, of both the Romans and the Corinthians. For indeed both planted also in our Corinth, and likewise taught us; and likewise they taught together also in Italy, and were martyred on the same occasion. Paul was beheaded at Rome itself, and Peter likewise was crucified. This story is accredited by the attachment, which prevails to this day, of the names of Peter and Paul to the cemeteries there. I can point out the memorials of the apostles. For if you would go to the Vatican, or to the Ostian Way, you will find the memorials of those who founded this church.'

13 Who is Jesus? The Gospels

This unit explains what a Gospel is.

St Paul's letters expect the reader to know about Jesus. That is because Paul or another missionary had already told them about him. The people that Paul wrote to were already Christian believers.

When St Paul arrived in a town where no one had yet heard of Jesus he would have to think how to introduce him. If there was a Jewish community, that was not difficult. Jews had the Torah. It would be possible to persuade the Jews to look at their scriptures. St Paul could try to persuade them that they pointed to Jesus, who was the Messiah. To non-Jews, who did not even know of the Torah, and had never heard of the Messiah, preachers would begin by telling them that Jesus was a man sent by God. He was someone who did good, healing the sick and teaching people how to live the kind of lives that God expected of them. They would then come to the tricky part: Jesus was wrongly accused of being a threat to the Roman state, he was executed, and three days later he appeared again, alive! Some listeners would take a lot of convincing. That is where the Apostles could describe their own personal experiences. 'We were there, we saw it, the arrest, the mock trial, the execution, and we have met the risen Jesus!' they would say.

Nero's persecution may have only taken place in Rome, but it silenced Jesus' most famous disciples, Peter and Paul. There was a need to ensure that what they had taught about Jesus was safe. A great decision was made to write the message down before it was forgotten and before other stories slipped in which were not to be trusted.

The Gospels

There are four books in the New Testament which are called **Gospels**. They contain the message which missionaries like Paul preached. Of course, the story is not exactly as they would have told it. The Gospels are books. They have an introduction and a conclusion. They are carefully planned so that the story, the plot, unfolds in a way which will help the reader to understand the book.

Each Gospel introduces Jesus. It then describes some incidents in his life, meeting with people, teaching, healing someone, but the stories are never full descriptions. Usually the incident is left incomplete; there is no mention of what happened to the healed person on the next day or a week later. The writer seems less interested in what happened than in what the story meant. Questions are raised which centre on one main issue: 'Who is this Jesus?' The answer is given many times. He is the Messiah, but that is not the whole story: he is the Son of God. Sometimes the challenge is thrown down very dramatically. For example, Mark describes a discussion that Jesus had with his disciples.

> 'Jesus and his disciples set out for the village of Caesarea Philippi, and on the way he asked his disciples, "Who do people say I am?" They answered, "Some say John the Baptist, others Elijah, others one of the prophets." "And you," he asked, "who do you say that I am?" Peter replied: "You are the Messiah." Then he gave them strict orders not to tell anyone about him; and he began to teach them that the Son of Man had to endure great suffering, and to be rejected by the elders, chief priests, and scribes; to be put to death; and to rise again three days afterwards. He spoke about it plainly. At this Peter took hold of him and began to rebuke him. But Jesus, turning and looking at his disciples, rebuked Peter. "Out of my sight, Satan!" he said, "you think only as men think, not as God thinks."'
>
> (*Mark* 8:27–33)

Mark didn't write this just because the incident happened. Readers are asked to stand in the position of the disciples. It asks them, 'Who do *you* say Jesus is?' That is Mark's great question. He goes on to warn the reader to prepare for the **crucifixion** and resurrection. Even this is more than a preparation for the next part of the story. It is a statement that this was God's plan. The disciples didn't

A modern painting of the crucifixion by Salvador Dali.

understand it. The reader is asked, 'Do you? Do you believe it?'

'Gospel' is an anglo-saxon word meaning 'good news'. The good news is that the promised Messiah has come. He is Jesus. The four Gospels say what the good news is. They ask readers who have never heard of Jesus to become his disciples. They help those who are already Christians to understand Jesus' message. They were written to persuade people to believe and were also read by people who were already Christians.

Christians believe that they can still know Jesus. For them he is alive. For them the Gospels are not stories about Jesus, but a way of meeting him now, in a spiritual way.

Why are there four Gospels?

One of many answers to this question is that the writers had different readers in mind. They wrote their story to fit the needs of their particular Christian community.

Matthew, *Mark* and *Luke* are very similar, because Matthew and Luke used accounts found in *Mark* and also other material which scholars call 'Q'. This is the initial letter of a German word, 'Quelle', which means 'source'. It may have been **oral teaching**, as no copy of it has ever been found. *John* uses very different material. The four Gospel writers are called **evangelists**.

NEW WORDS

Crucifixion a Roman method of execution; the victim was nailed to a wooden cross

Evangelist writer of one of the New Testament Gospels

Gospel good news; a book which describes the ministry, death and resurrection of Jesus

Oral teaching teaching passed on by word of mouth, not written down

Part of one of Paul's synagogue sermons

'We are here to give you the good news that God, who made the promise to the fathers, has fulfilled it for the children by raising Jesus from the dead, as indeed it stands written in the second Psalm: "You are my son; this day I have begotten you." Again, that he raised him from the dead, never to be subjected to corruption, he declares in these words: "I will give you the blessings promised to David, holy and sure." This is borne out by another passage: "You will not let your faithful servant suffer corruption." As for David, when he had served the purpose of God in his own generation, he died and was gathered to his fathers, and suffered corruption; but the one whom God raised up did not suffer corruption. You must understand, my brothers, it is through him that forgiveness of sins is now being proclaimed to you.' (*Acts* 13:32–38)

14 Parables

This unit explains what a **parable** is.

Parables

Jesus spent about three years travelling with his closest disciples. Sometimes they might stay with other disciples such as Mary, Martha and their brother Lazarus, or with Zacchaeus, a tax collector of Jericho. Wherever they went, Jesus taught people how they should live if they wanted to keep the spirit of the Torah and be his disciples.

A Jewish teaching method was to tell a challenging story and ask the listeners to work out what it meant. It seemed to be about ordinary, everyday things but its meaning was spiritual or moral. It was called a parable. Jesus once said:

> 'Listen! A sower went out to sow. And it happened that as he sowed, some of the seed fell along the footpath; and the birds came and ate it up. Some fell on rocky ground, where it had little soil, and it sprouted quickly because it had no depth of earth; but when the sun rose it was scorched and as it had no root it withered away. Some fell among thistles; and the thistles grew up and choked the corn, and it produced no crop. And some of the seed fell into good soil, where it came up and grew, and produced a crop; and the yield was thirtyfold, sixtyfold, even a hundredfold.' (*Mark* 4:3–9)

The parable of the lost coin

'Or suppose a woman who has ten silver coins loses one of them – what does she do? She lights a lamp, sweeps her house, and looks carefully everywhere until she finds it. When she finds it, she calls her friends and neighbours together, and says to them, "I am so happy I found the coin I lost. Let us celebrate!" In the same way, I tell you, the angels of God rejoice over one sinner who repents.' (*Luke* 15:8–10)

The other gospels contain many parables. Perhaps the most famous parable which Jesus told is this one.

The story of the lost son

> 'There was a man who had two sons; and the younger said to his father, "Father, give me my share of the property". So he divided his estate between them. A few days later the younger son turned all of his share into cash and left home for a distant country, where he squandered it on dissolute living. He had spent it all, when a famine fell upon that country and he began to be in need. So he went and attached himself to one of the local landowners, who sent him to his farm to mind the pigs. He would have been thankful to fill his belly with the pods that the pigs were eating, but nobody gave him anything. Then he came to his senses: "How many of my father's hired servants have more food than they can eat," he said, "and here am I, starving to death! I will go to my father, and say to him, 'Father, I have sinned against God and against you; I am no longer fit to be called your son; treat me as one of your hired servants.'" So he set out for his father's house. But while he was still a long way off his father saw him, and his heart went out to him; he ran towards him, flung his arms around him, and kissed him. The son said, "Father, I have sinned against God and against you; I am no longer fit to be called your son." But the father said to his servants, "Quick! fetch the robe, the best we have, and put it on him; put rings on his fingers and sandals on his feet. Bring the fatted calf and kill it, and let us celebrate with a feast. For this son of mine was dead and has come to life; he was lost and is found." And the festivities began.
>
> Now the elder son had been out on the farm; and on his way back, as he approached the house, he heard music and dancing. He called one of the servants and asked what it meant. The servant told him: "Your brother has come home, and your father has killed the fatted calf because he has him back safe and sound." But he was angry and refused to go in. His father came out and pleaded with him; but he retorted,

'You know how I have slaved for you all these years; I never disobeyed your orders; yet you never gave me as much as a kid, to celebrate with my friends. But now that this son of yours turns up, after running through your money with his women, you kill the fatted calf for him."

"My son," said the father, "you are always with me, and everything that I have is yours. How could we fail to celebrate this happy day? Your brother here was dead and has come back to life; he was lost and has been found."'

(*Luke* 15:11–32)

This parable comes as one of a group of three. The first is about a lost sheep, the second about a lost coin. This one is about a lost son.

When Jesus told the story his listeners would have been Jews. The message to them might have been that God, the father, cares for good Jews who keep the Torah and 'lost ones' who do not. The 'good' ones should be forgiving, as God is. When Luke wrote down the story there were Jews and Gentiles in the church. The Jews might be the elder brother and the Gentiles the younger one. The message might be that Jews and Christians should realise that they are both equal in God's eyes. He has no favourites.

NEW WORD

Parable a story, with a meaning or lesson

Jesus' explanation of the parable of the sower

'The sower sows the word. With some the seed falls along the footpath; no sooner have they heard it than Satan comes and carries off the word.... With others the seed falls on rocky ground; as soon as they hear the word, they accept it with joy, but it strikes no root in them;...and when there is trouble...on account of the word, they quickly lose faith. With others the seed falls among thistles; they hear the word, but worldly cares and the false glamour of wealth and evil desires of all kinds come in and choke the word, and it proves barren. But there are some with whom the seed is sown on good soil; they accept the word when they hear it, and they bear fruit thirtyfold, sixtyfold or a hundredfold.' (*Mark* 4:13–20)

Sowing seed by hand.

15 Signs of the Kingdom: the miracles

This unit explains the significance of the signs of Jesus, which are often called miracles.

All the Gospels contain many stories like this one.

> 'A man who was paralysed was brought to Jesus. Four men were carrying him, but because of the crowd they could not get him near. So they made an opening in the roof over the place where Jesus was, and when they had broken through they lowered the bed on which the paralysed man was lying. When he saw their faith, Jesus said to the man, "My son, your sins are forgiven".
>
> Now there were some scribes sitting there, thinking to themselves, "How can this fellow talk like that? It is blasphemy! Who but God can forgive sins?" Jesus knew at once what they were thinking, and said to them, "Why do you harbour such thoughts? Is it easier to say to this paralysed man, 'your sins are forgiven,' or to say, 'Stand up, take your bed, and walk'? But to convince you that the Son of Man has authority on earth to forgive sins" – he turned to the paralysed man – "I say to you, stand up, take your bed, and go home." And he got up, and at once took his bed and went out in full view of them all, so that they were astounded and praised God. "Never before," they said, "have we seen anything like this." ' (*Mark* 2:1–12)

We might ask *how* Jesus managed to heal the man. This question cannot be answered. If we read the passage carefully we can discover that only one question can actually be answered. It is: *why* did Jesus heal the man? Jesus made the man better to show that he had the right to forgive sins. Actions speak louder than words, so Jesus didn't just say, 'Your sins are forgiven', and leave the man lying on the stretcher. The scribes understood what he was saying. They were not pleased because Jesus was claiming a power which belonged only to God. He was behaving in a Messianic way. Look back to the words of *Isaiah*, which Jesus read in the synagogue at Nazareth (page 10).

Mark asks readers what conclusion they draw. Is Jesus the one sent by God? Has he been given the power to forgive sins? Is he a worker of tricks who cons people into believing in him? The crowd seem to have gone away remembering what they had seen more than what Jesus had said. The scribes refused to believe what Jesus had said. The miracle story, like the parables, is a challenge. Perhaps 'miracle' is not a very good word to use. The Greek word in the Gospels means signs, not wonders. That is why 'Signs of the Kingdom' has been used in the title of this unit. Jesus often spoke about the coming of the Kingdom of God. He suggested that his mission marked the beginning of God's rule.

Sometimes the meaning of the sign may be lost upon modern readers. For example, one evening Jesus fed 5,000 men and women who had come to listen to him.

> 'It was already getting late, and his disciples came to him and said, "This is a remote place; send the people off to the farms and villages round about, to buy themselves something to eat." "Give them something to eat yourselves," he answered. They replied, "Are we to go and

Houses with flat roofs are almost as common in modern Israel as they were in Jesus' day.

A silver denarius coin of Tiberius. He was the Roman emperor when Jesus was crucified.

spend 200 denarii to provide them with food?" "How many loaves have you?" he asked. "Go and see." They told him, "Five, and two fish." He ordered them to sit down in groups. Then, taking the five loaves and the two fish, he looked up to heaven, said the blessing, broke the loaves, and gave them to the disciples to distribute. He also divided the two fish among them. They all ate and were satisfied; and 12 baskets were filled with what was left of the bread and fish. Those who ate the loaves numbered 5,000 men.' (*Mark* 6:34–44)

People always want to try to explain what really happened. Sometimes the suggestion is made that one of the crowd brought out the food he had brought and shared it with the rest. Others, put to shame, took out their food and did the same thing. Does the account suggest that anything like this happened? This is not a story about sharing food with people in need. Jewish readers would know what the message was. It was that when the Messiah came to establish the rule of God he would call everyone to a great banquet. The feeding of the 5,000 was a sign that the Messiah had arrived. Another version of the story in *John's Gospel* said that this happened at the time of Passover. It was at one Passover meal that Jesus ate a last supper with his disciples. The meal which Christians celebrate in remembrance of it looks back to that supper and forward to the great banquet which, they believe, is still to come.

Jesus' clue to understanding miracles

Mark mentions the temptation of Jesus before he began preaching but gives no details. *Matthew* (4:1–11) and *Luke* (4:1–12) provide them. They say that Jesus was invited to turn stones into bread in order to feed himself; to worship the devil, in return for which the devil would give him the power to rule the world; and to jump off the Temple roof, to discover whether he really had the power which he was supposed to possess. If he had such power he would come to no harm. Jesus refused to use his power selfishly, to use it to win political power, and to impress people. If Jesus was true to himself he could never perform miracles which went against these principles.

Jesus did not claim unique healing powers

'Jesus was driving out a demon which was dumb; and when the demon had come out, the dumb man began to speak. The people were astonished, but some of them said, "It is by Beelzebul prince of demons that he drives the demons out." Others, by way of a test, demanded of him a sign from heaven. But he knew what was in their minds, and said, "Every kingdom divided against itself is laid waste, and a divided household falls. And if Satan is divided against himself, how can his kingdom stand – since, as you claim, I drive out the demons by Beelzebul? If it is by Beelzebul that I drive out demons, by whom do your own people drive them out?"'

(*Luke* 11:14–19)

16 The resurrection stories

This unit is about the most important event of the New Testament: the resurrection of Jesus.

For Christians the most important part of each Gospel is the section which describes the resurrection of Jesus. That is because the whole of Christian faith depends on that greatest sign of God's power. St Paul put it like this:

> 'If the dead are not raised, it follows that Christ was not raised; and if Christ was not raised your faith has nothing in it and you are still in your old state of sin.' (*1 Corinthians* 15:16–17)

The Christians in Corinth must have been throwing doubt upon the resurrection of Jesus to make Paul write those words. He then describes a tradition of appearances which had become established by the time he was writing his letter. Paul adds some which are not in the gospels.

> 'First and foremost, I handed on to you the tradition I had received: that Christ died for our sins according to the scriptures; that he was buried; that he was raised to life on the third day, in accordance with the scriptures; and that he appeared to Cephas and afterwards to the Twelve. Then he appeared to over 500 of our brothers at once, most of whom are still alive, though some have died. Then he appeared to James and afterwards to all the apostles.'
> (*1 Corinthians* 15:3–80)

Each of the four Gospels has different resurrection stories to tell. This is probably because the communities for which they were written cherished the accounts which they had received from the Apostles who had witnessed them. All four agree, however, that the first followers to be told that Jesus had risen from the dead were women. In *John* (20:14–18) a woman, Mary of Magdala, is the first person to whom Jesus chose to show himself, even though Peter and another disciple had seen the empty tomb.

Jesus may have been buried in a tomb like this, with a stone that rolled across it to seal the entrance.

On the road to Emmaus

One of the most vivid accounts of Jesus appearing to followers on the day of his resurrection is in *Luke*. Two dispirited disciples were on their way from Jerusalem to a village called Emmaus. They were arguing about the women's news and the fact that other disciples who had gone to the tomb found it empty. Someone caught up with them as they walked. He asked them what they were discussing. They told him about Jesus and their hope he was the Messiah. Their companion began to refer to passages in the Hebrew scriptures which pointed to a suffering Messiah. They doubted still. By evening they reached their village. They asked the man to stay with them. He agreed. Then something remarkable happened. Luke says:

> 'When he sat down with them at table, he took bread and said the blessing; he broke the bread and offered it to them. Then their eyes were opened, and they recognised him; but he vanished from their sight.' (*Luke* 24:30–31)

Luke adds one more story. When the couple got back to Jerusalem they gave their account and heard that Jesus had also appeared to Peter. As they were talking Jesus appeared and stood among them.

'Startled and terrified, they were afraid that they were seeing a ghost, but he said, "Why are you so perturbed? Why do such doubts arise in your minds? Look at my hands and feet. It is I myself. Touch me and see; no ghost has flesh and bones as you can see I have."'

To convince them he asked for food and ate a piece of fish. He then reminded them of the teaching he had given them about the suffering and resurrection of the Messiah being predicted in the Torah.

Mark's account of the resurrection

Mark's Gospel describes Mary of Magdala, Mary the mother of James, and Salome arriving at the tomb to anoint the body of Jesus (something there would be no time to do on the Friday, as the Sabbath would begin almost as soon as Jesus was dead). They were wondering how they would manage to remove the stone from the entrance when they saw that it had already been rolled back.

'They went into the tomb, where they saw a young man sitting on the right-hand side, wearing a white robe; and they were dumbfounded. But he said to them, "Do not be alarmed; you are looking for Jesus of Nazareth who was crucified. He has been raised; he is not here. Look, there is the place where they laid him. But go and say to his disciples and to Peter: 'He is going ahead of you into Galilee; there you will see him as he told you.'" Then they went out and ran away from the tomb, trembling with amazement. They said nothing to anyone; they were afraid.' (*Mark* 16:4–8)

The Gospel ends just like that. Why did Mark stop at that point? If, however, you look at a copy of Mark, you will see that some manuscripts add another sentence to the verse and some another section (verses 9 to 19). It seems that very soon after Mark had finished his work Christians were not satisfied with the abrupt stop at verse eight.

Another ending may be *John*, chapter 21. If you read it carefully you may be able to see how it fits in with *Mark* 16:1–8. If you look at *John* 20:30 it seems as though the author is finishing Mark's account.

For some people these kinds of questions are fascinating, almost like detective work. However, the question that matters, as St Paul said, is whether Jesus really rose from the dead or not.

Christians may disagree on what happened. Some believe that the Emmaus road account was of a sudden realization of what Jesus had been teaching. The two disciples were trying to handle their grief and disappointment as they walked away from Jerusalem. Jesus' teachings kept returning to their minds and, as they sat down to supper and broke bread and blessed it as Jesus had done, they suddenly realized that he was with them, just as Christians today believe that he is. In other words, 'the penny dropped'. Other Christians believe that Jesus actually appeared physically to the travellers.

Arguments about how the resurrection happened and what happened could go on till the end of time. Christian faith is based on the belief that Jesus lives now and gives life and hope to his disciples today as much as he did 2,000 years ago. It convinces them that he was not merely a good man who was unjustly killed; he was God.

The third appearance of Jesus to his disciples by the sea of Galilee

'After breakfast Jesus said to Simon Peter, "Simon son of John, do you love me more than these others?" "Yes, Lord," he answered, "you know that I love you." "Then feed my lambs," he said. A second time he asked, "Simon son of John, do you love me?" "Yes, Lord, you know I love you." "Then tend my sheep." A third time he said, "Simon son of John, do you love me?" Peter was hurt that he asked him a third time, "Do you love me?" "Lord," he said, "you know everything; you know I love you." Jesus said, "Then feed my sheep."' (*John* 21:15–17)

17 The Book of Revelation

This unit is about the last and strangest New Testament book.

One book of the New Testament is different from all the rest: the *Book of Revelation*. It is the description of a great vision given to John who is sometimes said to have been one of the twelve disciples and the writer of the fourth Gospel. He was in exile on the island of Patmos because, as he wrote, 'I had preached God's word and borne my testimony to Jesus' (1:9). Today he would be called a prisoner of conscience. His book contains some fantastic pictures in words. Here is one example:

> 'I had a vision; a door stood open in heaven, and the voice that I had first heard speaking to me like a trumpet said, "Come up here and I will show you what must take place hereafter." At once the Spirit came upon me. There in heaven stood a throne. On it sat One whose appearance was like jasper or a cornelian, and round it was a rainbow, bright as an emerald. In a circle around this throne were 24 other thrones, and on them were seated 24 elders, robed in white and wearing golden crowns...
>
> 'Day and night unceasingly they sing: "Holy, holy, holy, is the sovereign Lord of all, who was, and is, and is to come!"' (4:1–4 and 8)

The *Book of Revelation* seems full of riddles but in chapter 13 there is the biggest puzzle of all. It describes two beasts. First one rises out of the sea, wages war on God's people and defeats them. Then another beast appears who sets up an image to the first one and makes everyone worship it. In verse 18 the author gives the beast a number, not a name. It is 666, which represents the numerical value of the name. *Revelation* is about the end of history when Jesus, the lamb of God, will judge and rule the earth. Those who stand around God's throne sing:

> '"Worthy is the lamb who was slain, to receive power and wealth, wisdom and might, honour and glory and praise!"
>
> 'Then I heard all created things, in heaven, on earth, under the earth, and in the sea, crying:
>
> '"Praise and honour, glory and might, to him who sits on the throne and to the lamb forever!"' (5:12–13)

One of the last of the visions is of a new heaven and earth with a new Jerusalem in it which comes down from heaven.

> 'I saw a new heaven and a new earth, for the first heaven and the first earth had vanished, and there was no longer any sea. I saw the holy city, new Jerusalem, coming down out of heaven from God, made ready like a bride adorned for her husband. I heard a loud voice proclaiming from the throne: "Now God has his dwelling with humankind! He will dwell among them and they shall be his people, and God himself will be with them. He will wipe every tear away from their eyes. There shall be an end to death, and to mourning and crying and pain, for the old order has passed away!"' (21:1–4)

The meaning of *Revelation*

For hundreds of years Christians have puzzled and argued about the meaning of this book. The beast's number, 666, has been worked

Catacombs in Rome.

The code read:

'A(autokrator)	KA	I (sar)	D	O	M	E	T(ianos)	S	E	B(astos)	G	E(rmanikos).	
1	21	10	4	70	40	5	300	200	5	2	3	6	= 666

out to apply to such men as popes, Napoleon and Adolf Hitler. However, it probably refers to the emperor who was ruling when the book was written, Domitian. He had grown up in Nero's court and learned something of his ways. Towards the end of his reign, in 96CE, he persecuted Jews and Christians for refusing to worship him as God, and his cruelty towards any subjects who disagreed with him led to his assassination. The number 666 may be a coded way of indicating his official name which was Autokrator Kaiser Dometianos Sebastos Germanikos. (*See table above.*)

The numbers are the values of some of the Greek letters. In Greek A (α)=1, but the Greek alphabet is not the same as the English one. G (γ) is the third letter, for example, and E (ε) is the fifth.

Like the *Book of Daniel* in the Old Testament, *Revelation* is not intended to be about the distant future. It is telling persecuted people to keep the faith.

The message, in a nutshell, is that the evil-doers will soon perish and God's rule will replace theirs. Its meaning must have been clear to its first readers, the church on the mainland, to which it was smuggled. After the troubled times ended the book was neglected and its original meaning forgotten. It only found a place in the Bible because John, the author, was thought to be the writer of *John's Gospel*.

The final triumph of good over evil has not yet taken place so some Christians interpret *Revelation* as relating to the future. They may lose sight of the comfort and spiritual worth of the book for Christians in any age, just as those who disagree with them may make the mistake of ignoring it altogether.

Revelation ends with a promise from Jesus: 'Yes, I am coming soon!' To which John replies: 'Amen. Come, Lord Jesus!' and adds, to his readers, now as then: 'The grace of the Lord Jesus be with all.'

The second coming of Jesus, his return, is something which has always troubled Christians. Remember there were people in Thessalonica who gave up their jobs to prepare for it (page 19). What the new heaven and earth will be like and how it will happen is a mystery but all Christians believe that the story isn't complete. The best is yet to come!

A silver denarius coin of Emperor Domitian, the beast of the Book of Revelation.

Another vision of the New Jerusalem:

'I saw no temple in the city, for its temple was the sovereign Lord God and the Lamb. The city did not need the sun or the moon to shine on it, for the glory of God gave it light, and its lamp was the Lamb. By its light shall the nations walk, and to it the kings of the earth shall bring their splendour. The gates of the city shall never be shut by day, nor will there be any night there.'

(*Revelation* 21:22–25)

18 The search for ancient manuscripts

This unit tells the story of the search for early copies of books of the Bible.

No original manuscripts of a letter from St Paul, of a gospel, or of any book of the Bible exist. There may be many reasons for this.

First, we have already seen that long before the time of Jesus, Jews had translated the Torah from Hebrew into Greek. Some Jews may have believed that the word of God must always be kept in the original Hebrew, but many did not. The Jewish converts to Christianity were not concerned about the Hebrew text. It was what the Bible said that mattered most to them.

Secondly, the New Testament grew little by little over about 200 years. During this time Christians were a minority group in the Roman Empire. They could not preserve their writings perfectly. Some got lost as people fled from persecution, or were destroyed on the orders of persecuting emperors.

A third reason was that Christians were not to be found in only one part of the Roman world. There were Christians in every country from Britain to Spain, Egypt, and Armenia.

Emperor Constantine declared that Christianity was a legal religion in 313CE. Before that, Christians had often been persecuted, especially by Diocletian, whom Constantine replaced. Constantine began to support the church. Now Christian leaders could meet legally; he even paid their expenses. He also encouraged fine copies of the Bible to be written for use in the great churches. Perhaps one of these copies is the **Codex** Sinaiticus in the British Museum. It is called this because it was found on Mount Sinai, in the **monastery** of St Catherine.

Finding the Codex Sinaiticus

Constantin Tischendorff, a German, visited the monastery in 1844 and entered it in the usual way, by being hauled up in a wicker basket. To keep him warm the monks provided him with fuel for the fire in his room. He saw that this was **vellum**, treated animal skins. When he looked at them he realized that they were part of a very old, hand-written copy of the Bible. He persuaded the monks to let him take some of the sheets back to Germany. In 1859 he returned to the monastery and this time he was shown more manuscripts. Among them was the rest of the one that had been intended for his fire. He eventually managed to see all of it. He got the monks to send it to their sister monastery in Cairo, where he copied it. There were 199 pages of the Old Testament in Greek, all the New Testament, and a letter by the Apostle Barnabas. The Tsar of Russia heard of the treasure which the monks had in their monastery. They made him a present of the manuscript. In 1933 the Soviet government sold the Codex to the British Museum for £100,000. It is now on display there. Tischendorff had saved the earliest complete copy known of the New Testament but he could never stop wondering how many other manuscripts had gone up in smoke!

The Dead Sea Scrolls

Occasionally, in countries like Israel, where the dry climate preserves ancient things well, archaeologists find pieces of the Bible. One of the most famous recent discoveries was in Israel in 1947. According to one account, an Arab boy was looking after a flock of sheep and goats. He threw stones into some of the caves in the nearby hills. Usually he heard the sound of the stones bouncing off the walls, but this time he heard the noise of breaking pottery. Inside the cave were large jars containing scrolls. They had been carefully hidden to save them from the Romans in 66CE, when there was a great Jewish revolt against their Roman rulers. The owners of the scrolls never returned to the caves. They were probably killed. The scrolls lay unclaimed for almost 1,900 years. When scholars eventually got their hands on them they found that they included most of the books of the Torah in Hebrew and were 1,000 years older than any other existing copies. They are known as the Dead Sea Scrolls.

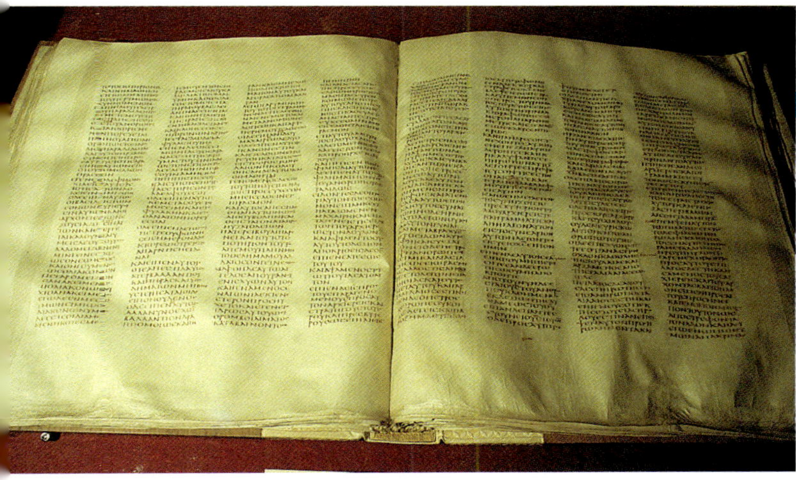

The Codex Sinaiticus in the British Museum. It may be one of the Bibles which Emperor Constantine had made for the great churches.

Discoveries, like those of the Codex Sinaiticus and the Dead Sea Scrolls, have reassured Christians that the texts which were used by translators such as William Tyndale were reliable (see page 43). They only got a word wrong here and there.

Joseph's coat

Sometimes knowledge of ancient languages matters more than an accurate text. For example, the story of Joseph's 'coat of many colours' has been made into a popular musical, 'Joseph and his Amazing Technicolour Dreamcoat,' but modern translations of *Genesis* 37:3 mention 'a long robe with sleeves'. Scholars know ancient Hebrew better now than they did when they produced the Authorised Version in 1611. The robe was a sign that Jacob had chosen Joseph to be his heir, rather than one of the older brothers. They were not jealous of a pretty jacket, but of knowing that one day their young brother would boss them about!

Books, chapters, and verses

Throughout this book chapters and verses have been mentioned. The Jewish scriptures were divided into chapters in about 900CE. The New Testament was divided into chapters by an Archbishop of Canterbury called Stephen Langton. Verses did not exist in the New Testament until 1551, when a French printer, Robert Estienne, introduced them. Rabbi Isaac Nathan had already divided the Jewish Scriptures into verses in about 1440CE.

It must be remembered that the whole Bible seems to have been written in scroll form! Someone had the brilliant idea of binding all the sections of a book together down the spine instead of stitching them end to end. Who it was no one knows, but whoever it was made life easier for everyone! Imagine how difficult it must have been to find a place in one of the longer books of the Bible before it was written in pages and when there were no divisions into chapters or verses. The use of pages also made it possible to write on both sides of a piece of parchment so books could be less bulky than they had been before.

NEW WORDS

Codex a manuscript written in book form, rather than as a scroll

Monastery place where people who have taken special vows live as a religious community

Vellum writing material made from animal skins

The coat of many colours

'Because Joseph was a child of his old age, Israel loved him best of all his sons, and made him a long robe with sleeves. When his brothers saw that their father loved him best, it aroused their hatred and they had nothing but harsh words for him. Joseph had a dream, and when he told it to his brothers, their hatred of him became still greater. He said to them, "Listen to this dream I had. We were out in the field binding sheaves, when all at once my sheaf rose and stood upright, and your sheaves gathered round an bowed in homage before my sheaf." His brothers retorted, "Do you think that you will indeed be king over us and rule us?" and they hated him still more.' (*Genesis* 37:2–8)

19 Canon, creeds, controversies

This unit explains how the Bible library was completed.

If Christians living a year or even ten years after the death and resurrection of Jesus had been asked what their Bible was they would have replied, 'the Torah'. However, the content of the Torah was uncertain. It was not until about 90CE that a gathering of rabbis agreed upon the books that should be included in the sections called Prophets (**Nevi'im**) and Writings (**Ketubim**). Christians have never accepted the Jewish collection of books exactly. Protestant Christians include the same books as the Jews in their Old Testament. Roman Catholics include extra books, known as the **Apocrypha**, which are in the Greek version of the Torah.

The Septuagint

About 200 years before the time of Jesus there were Jews living in Egypt who no longer spoke or read Hebrew. They used Greek instead, so it was decided to translate the Torah into Greek. It is said that 70 scholars were brought to Egypt to make the translation. They did not work together, yet they came up with identical copies. This is a way of saying that God inspired them and that the Greek translation is as reliable as the original Hebrew. The story gave the translation its name, Septuagint. It means 70, and is sometimes written LXX (70 in Roman numerals) as an abbreviation.

It was this Greek translation of the Jewish Scriptures that the Christians of Rome, Corinth and the other places that St Paul went to would have used in worship. Even after St Paul had written all his letters and the four Gospels had appeared, Christians might still have said that the Torah was their Bible, but with less certainty. They would have wanted to say that there was something special about the Christian writings of St Paul and others. Eventually they may have read them in their services. Certainly their preachers would have quoted large parts of them in sermons. When Christians from one church visited another they would make a copy of any writing that they came across which was new to them and take it back to their home church. It would be listened to eagerly by members of the congregation, who might decide to include it in their collection of Christian writings. Sometimes, however, they might discuss the book, feel that it didn't quite match up to the teaching which they had received from the Apostles, and reject it.

The canon of the New Testament

In this way a **canon of scripture** developed by accident. The Greek word 'kanon' means 'reed' or 'cane' and refers to an ancient measuring rod. 'Canon of scripture' means the yard stick, or metre measure, by which the truth of Christian teaching can be measured. If someone taught something that was not in the scriptures, they were wrong.

There were some people in the early days of the church who said that Jesus was only a

This diagram lists the books of the New Testament. Remember that most of the Bible is made up of the Old Testament. Find out what percentage is Old Testament by looking at a Bible.

man: the best man who ever lived, perhaps, but not divine. Others refused to believe that Jesus could have been a man at all. The human body disgusted them. They could not believe that God could ever become man. The Jesus who walked in Galilee was a spirit. The crucifixion was a kind of trick. It didn't really happen. The writings of such believers would be rejected because they did not measure up to the yardstick of apostolic teaching.

Gradually the New Testament which Christians use today took shape, but it was not until 367CE that a famous bishop of Alexandria, Athanasius, mentioned them all in the order found in Bibles today. The list included in his Easter Letter and was intended to guide the reading of Christians in his **diocese** so that they would not be misled by false teaching. The New Testament was given its name to distinguish it from the Jewish Scriptures which became the Old Testament.

Creeds

Debates about which books were trustworthy went hand-in-hand with arguments about what Christians should believe. At first it was enough to say 'Jesus is Lord' or 'Jesus Christ, Son of God, Saviour'. Gradually, Christians decided that the meaning of these words should be given in more detail. All these statements of belief are called **creeds**. This comes from the Latin 'credo', meaning 'I believe'. It is often the first word of a creed.

Controversies

Instead of emphasising commitment, creeds came to be used to distinguish Christians whose views were considered to be correct from others, such as those who could not believe that Jesus could be both human and divine. People who held beliefs which differed from the creeds were called **heretics**. Often they were forced to leave the church, and their writings were destroyed. Sometimes their writings come to light and make headline news. In 1945 archaeologists found a book called the *Gospel of Thomas*. It was not like the Bible Gospels; it did not mention the crucifixion and resurrection, but it was a collection of teachings.

Sometimes writers have forged a book to put across their message. One of the most famous is the *Gospel of Barnabas*. It claims to be by St Paul's companion on his first missionary journey, but was actually written about 1,500 years later! The author may not have been a Christian.

NEW WORDS

Apocrypha books found in the Greek version of the Bible, but not in the Hebrew

Canon of scripture the agreed collection of books in the Bible

Creed statement of belief

Diocese group of churches presided over by a bishop

Heretic someone who holds views which are rejected by the majority

Ketubim writings, third section of the Jewish Scriptures

Nevi'im prophets, second section of the Jewish Scriptures

The Apostles' Creed

'I believe in God, the Father almighty, creator of heaven and earth.

'I believe in Jesus Christ, his only Son, our Lord. He was conceived by the power of the Holy Spirit and born of the Virgin Mary. He suffered under Pontius Pilate, was crucified, died, and was buried. He descended to the dead. On the third day he rose again. He ascended into heaven, and is seated at the right hand of the Father. He will come again to judge the living and the dead.

'I believe in the Holy Spirit, the holy catholic Church, the communion of saints, the forgiveness of sins, the resurrection of the body, and the life everlasting. Amen.'

20 Bible translations

This unit is the story of the Bible being translated into many languages.

Most of the Old Testament was written in Hebrew and the New Testament in Greek. However, the followers of Jesus have never believed there is a special, sacred language. The Septuagint was written to meet the needs of Jews who did not understand Hebrew (see page 40). This puzzling acrostic (word puzzle) was found in the ruins of the Roman city of Pompeii, which was destroyed by a volcanic eruption in 79CE. It may be evidence that Christians were using Latin in worship even before the New Testament was complete.

ROTAS
OPERA
TENET
AREPO
SATOR

If you look carefully at it, you may see a pattern inside it: the shape of a cross. A Christian, reading Latin, might make out two hidden words: PATER NOSTER. These are the first words of the Lord's Prayer in Latin. Keep N as your middle letter and see if you can rearrange the acrostic to make a cross with two PATER NOSTERs, one horizontal and the other vertical. Four letters are left: two As and two Os. They are the Latin equivalents of α and ω, alpha and omega, the first and last letters of the Greek alphabet. (In *Revelation*, Jesus is described as 'Alpha and Omega' – in 1:8, for example.) It is likely that the prayer which Jesus taught his disciples in Aramaic, their mother tongue, was being used in Latin within 40 years of Jesus' lifetime. (The same words have been found in other places, one being Cirencester in England.)

Eventually, Latin became the language of the church in Western Europe. A Latin translation, the **Vulgate**, was the only version people were allowed to use. As few people knew Latin and every book had to be written by hand, there was little chance of most people being able to read the Bible. The invention of printing altered all that. In 1456 Johann Gutenberg produced the first printed book in Europe, a Vulgate Bible.

Today the complete Bible can be read in over 300 languages, and the New Testament in 695. Sometimes, however, governments have discouraged translations. King Henry VIII (who ruled 1509–47) wanted it to remain in Latin so that the common people, who did not know Latin, had to be taught by an approved clergyman. Henry knew that a preacher called John Purvey had made an English translation in about 1388 and that this had led some people to doubt church teachings. King Henry himself had challenged the authority of the Pope, but he did not want his subjects to dispute the authority of their king!

An early printing press.

William Tyndale

Some people thought that anyone who could read English should be able to read the Bible, so they translated it into English. William Tyndale was one of these people. He knew that King Henry would try to have him arrested so he fled to the Netherlands for safety. He translated the New Testament into English in 1525. Smugglers brought the copies to London hidden in bales of wool. The Bishop of London tried to confiscate them. There is even a story that someone sold the Bishop large quantities of Tyndale's

New Testament, which were then burnt. However, the seller had been one of Tyndale's men. The money was used to buy better printing presses and produce more and better translations! The bishop had been tricked! Eventually, Tyndale was caught and burned to death in 1536. But in 1539 Henry VIII permitted an English Bible to be placed in every church, chained to a wall. The first five books of the Old Testament and the whole New Testament of this version were taken from the translation which Tyndale had made!

The most famous English version of the Bible is probably the Authorised Version which King James I of England (James VI of Scotland) ordered to be translated in 1611. It was in everyday English but today many people find it hard to read, so new translations have been made.

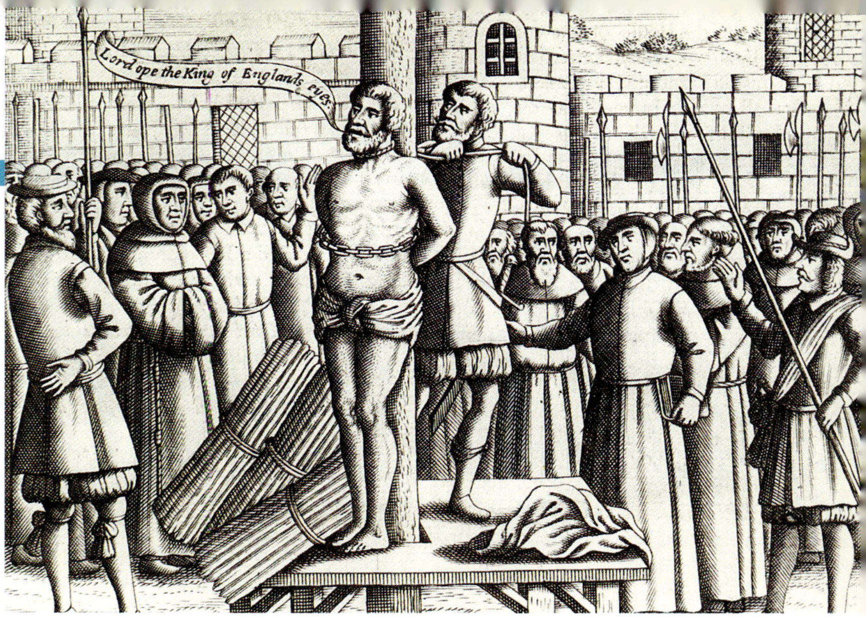

The execution of William Tyndale.

NEW WORD

Vulgate Latin version of the Bible, translated by St Jerome

Old customs die hard

This version of the Lord's Prayer, the prayer which Jesus taught his disciples and which many Christians say daily, is even older than the Authorised Version. It reads:

> 'Our Father, which art in heaven, hallowed be thy name. Thy kingdom come. Thy will be done, in earth as it is in heaven. Give us this day our daily bread, and forgive us our trespasses, as we forgive them that trespass against us. And lead us not into temptation; but deliver us from evil.' (*Matthew* 6:9–13)

It was used in the Book of Common Prayer of 1549 and is Tyndale's translation. Modern forms of the prayer are used in some churches, but they are not yet popular.

In the 20th century governments in Eastern Europe and China banned the Bible. Christians who owned copies were imprisoned. Some individuals and Christian organizations smuggled copies into these countries in the same way that Bibles were taken into England centuries ago.

St Paul's famous passage on love

'I may speak in tongues of men or of angels, but if I have no love, I am a sounding gong or a clanging cymbal. I may have the gift of prophecy and the knowledge of every hidden truth; I may have faith enough to move mountains; but if I have no love, I am nothing. I may give all I possess to the needy, I may give my body to be burnt, but if I have no love, I gain nothing by it. Love is patient and kind. Love envies no one, is never boastful, never conceited, never rude; love is never selfish, never quick to take offence. Love keeps no score of wrongs, takes no pleasure in the sins of others, but delights in the truth. There is nothing love cannot face; there is no limit to its faith, its hope, its endurance. Love will never come to an end. Prophecies will cease; tongues of ecstasy will fall silent; knowledge will vanish. For our knowledge and our prophecy alike are partial, and the partial vanishes when wholeness comes.'

(*1 Corinthians* 13:1–10)

21 The Bible in worship

This unit is about the way Christians use the Bible in church.

Early Christian worship

Jesus and his disciples were Jews, so they worshipped in the Temple at festival times and on other days when they were in Jerusalem. On the Sabbath they attended the local synagogue wherever they happened to be. Some synagogues might have become Christian churches if the congregation accepted the teachings of Jesus. Most did not. Those Jews and non-Jews who became Christians would have had to find somewhere to meet. They probably used private houses. The new religion was illegal until 313CE and was not allowed to own property. Any Christian who let his house be used for worship might find it confiscated if a government informer had been in the congregation.

A hundred years after Jesus' day

What Christians do when they worship is always more important than the places where they do it. The 'church' is the community of believers. Buildings, even beautiful cathedrals, don't really matter! Here is a description of worship which was written in about 152CE. The author, Justin Martyr, who was executed in 163CE, was trying to persuade anyone who would bother to read what he wrote, including the Emperor, that Christianity was not a danger but a benefit to the Empire. He wrote:

> 'On the day which is called Sunday there is an assembly of all who live in cities or in country districts; and the records of the Apostles, or the writings of the Prophets, are read as long as we have time. Then the reader finishes, and the president speaks, teaching and encouraging us to copy these excellent things. Then we all rise and offer up our prayer, bread is brought and wine and water; the President offers up prayers and thanksgiving with all his strength; and the people give their assent by saying 'Amen'. There is a distribution and partaking by everyone of the eucharistic elements; they are sent by deacons to those who are not present.'
>
> (*Apology*, I:65–67. Documents Illustrative of the History of the Church, vol.1, BJ Kidd, SPCK, 1920, page 27.)

A Romanian Christian reading a Romanian Bible.

The Bible is used in most acts of Christian worship. In Britain, the Society of Friends (Quakers) sit in silence until the Holy Spirit, the spirit of God, prompts one of them to speak. However, there will be a Bible on the table in the centre of the room and it is very likely that anyone who does feel moved to speak will refer to the Bible. She or he may come forward and read a passage to the meeting.

At the other extreme are Christians of such groups as the Free Church of Scotland. Their worship is very biblical. They sing only rhyming versions of the *Psalms* of the Old Testament. These hymns were composed in 1650. The form of Bible which they use in worship is the King James Version. This is part of one of the hymns which they sing:

> 'The Lord's my shepherd, I'll not want;
> He makes me down to lie
> In pastures green; he leadeth me
> The quiet waters by.'

This is based on *Psalm* 23. Scots brought up on the *Psalter* of 1650 will have no difficulty in understanding the words. For many young people today they might almost seem to be in a foreign language.

The most common use of the Bible is in the readings or lessons which are read during services. There will always be a passage from the New Testament, usually from one of the Gospels. Often an Epistle will be read (that is, one of the letters of the New Testament), and there may be an Old Testament reading, too. Sometimes *Mary's Song*, the *Magnificat*, to use its Latin name, and *Simeon's Song*, the *Nunc Dimittis*, are sung. These can both be found in *Luke*, chapters one and two. Sermons, talks by the minister to the congregation, are often based on the Bible readings.

An open air service in Kenya.

Psalm 23

'The Lord is my shepherd; I lack for nothing.
He makes me lie down in green pastures,
he leads me to water where I may rest;
he revives my spirit;
for his name's sake he guides me in the right paths.
Even were I to walk through a valley of deepest darkness
I should fear no harm, for you are with me;
your shepherd's staff and crook afford me comfort.

'You spread a table for me in the presence of my enemies;
you have richly anointed my head with oil,
and my cup brims over.
Goodness and love unfailing will follow me
all the days of my life,
and I shall dwell in the house of the Lord
throughout the years to come.'

22 The Bible and Christian conduct

This unit is about the way the Bible helps Christians decide how to behave.

How Christians should behave is something which has troubled them since Jesus began teaching.

Jesus took two verses from the Torah, and told his disciples that the whole of his message was based on them. They were:

> 'Love the Lord your God with all your heart, with all your soul, and with all your mind',
> (*Deuteronomy* 6:5) and

> 'Love your neighbour as yourself'
> (*Leviticus* 19:18)

This wasn't enough for those who listened to Jesus. Once his friend Peter asked him: 'How often shall I forgive my brother if he sins against me?' Jesus replied:

> 'I do not say seven times [as the Torah taught], but 70 times seven' (*Matthew* 18:21–22)

A student of the Torah asked Jesus, 'Who is my neighbour?' Jesus answered him with a parable. He said:

> 'A man was on his way from Jerusalem to Jericho when he was set upon by robbers, who stripped him and beat him, and went off leaving him half dead. It happened that a priest was going down by the same road, and when he saw him went by on the other side. So too a **Levite** came to the place, and when he saw him went past on the other side. But a **Samaritan** who was going that way came upon him, and when he saw him was moved to pity. He went up and bandaged his wounds, bathing them with oil and wine. Then he lifted him on his own beast, brought him to an inn, and looked after him. Next day he produced two silver pieces and gave them to the innkeeper and said, "Look after him; and if you spend more, I will repay you on my way back." Which of these three do you think was neighbour to the man who fell among robbers?'
>
> 'He answered, "The one who showed him kindness." Jesus said to him, "Go and do as he did".' (*Luke* 10:30–37)

Making up one's mind

When Christians try to decide what they should do in particular situations, they are guided by the traditions of the church, by the Bible and by what they believe God is telling them to do in answer to their prayers. They tend to turn to the words of Jesus and his followers rather than the Old Testament, but they don't ignore it. The Ten Commandments, (*Exodus* 20:3–17) are obeyed by Christians, though they have replaced the Sabbath with Sunday. However, some Christians, called Seventh Day Adventists, still keep the Jewish Sabbath, not Sunday, as their holy day.

The way that Sunday should be kept is a matter upon which Christians disagree among themselves. Church attendance is something that all would regard as important. Many would avoid working or causing others to work. Some would play sports, others would not; some would go to the cinema, theatre,

The Reverend David Sheppard, Anglican Bishop of Liverpool. He played cricket for England, but stopped when Sunday cricket began.

discos, the seaside, others would choose to do things like reading, gardening, going for walks with the family. David Sheppard, who later became Bishop of Liverpool, played cricket for Sussex and England, but gave up when Sunday cricket began. Michael Jones, a New Zealand All Black rugby player, refused to play in Sunday games in the 1990 World Cup.

Jesus said: 'Love your enemies', (*Matthew* 5:43) and refused to fight the men who came to arrest him (*Matthew* 26:51–53), so some Christians refuse to serve in the armed forces. They are called Pacifists. Most Christians, however, will fight if they think the cause is a just one.

The attitude of the Bible to women is another area of Christian disagreement. The Eastern Orthodox and Roman Catholic Churches do not have women priests, but the Anglican Churches are discussing the issue. Those who oppose the ordination of women argue that Jesus had no women Apostles and that St Paul disapproved of women being Church leaders. Verses which they use are:

> 'As in all the congregations of God's people, women should keep silent at the meeting. They have no permission to talk'
> (*1 Corinthians* 14:34) and

> 'I do not permit women to teach or dictate to the men; they should keep quiet' (*1 Timothy* 2:12)

Those who support the ordination of women point out that Jesus did have women disciples, though not included in the twelve, that St Paul was writing at a time when the status of women in society was inferior, and that a new religion with women leaders could have attracted unwelcome gossip and rumour. They would say that today the Christian emphasis should be upon equality and justice. They draw attention to St Paul's words,

> 'There is no such thing as Jew and Greek, slave and freeman, male and female; for you are all one person in Christ Jesus' (*Galatians* 3:28)

What is good or bad often depends on the time and place. If Christians with no power had attacked slavery, and had women leaders, in addition to refusing to take oaths to the emperor they might have had an even harder time than they did. Today things are different. All human beings, including women, have equal rights under British law.

NEW WORDS

Levites assistants in worship in the Temple

Samaritan someone from the region of Samaria. Samaritans were not considered to be true Jews

Peace Testimony of the Society of Friends

'We utterly deny all outward wars and strife, and fighting with outward weapons, for any end, or under any pretence whatever; this is our testimony to the whole world. The Spirit of Christ by which we are guided is not changeable, so as once to command us from a thing as evil, and again to move unto it; and we certainly know, and testify to the world, that the spirit of Christ, which leads us into all truth, will never move us to fight and war against any man with outward weapons, neither for the kingdom of Christ, nor for the kingdoms of the world.'

(From *A Declaration from the Harmless and Innocent People of God, called Quakers*, presented to Charles II, 1660)

Index